IFIP Advances in Information and Communication Technology

453

Editor-in-Chief

Kai Rannenberg, Goethe University, Frankfurt, Germany

IFIP – The International Federation for Information Processing

IFIP was founded in 1960 under the auspices of UNESCO, following the First World Computer Congress held in Paris the previous year. An umbrella organization for societies working in information processing, IFIP's aim is two-fold: to support information processing within its member countries and to encourage technology transfer to developing nations. As its mission statement clearly states,

> IFIP's mission is to be the leading, truly international, apolitical organization which encourages and assists in the development, exploitation and application of information technology for the benefit of all people.

IFIP is a non-profitmaking organization, run almost solely by 2500 volunteers. It operates through a number of technical committees, which organize events and publications. IFIP's events range from an international congress to local seminars, but the most important are:

- The IFIPWorld Computer Congress, held every second year;
- Open conferences;
- Working conferences.

The flagship event is the IFIP World Computer Congress, at which both invited and contributed papers are presented. Contributed papers are rigorously refereed and the rejection rate is high.

As with the Congress, participation in the open conferences is open to all and papers may be invited or submitted. Again, submitted papers are stringently refereed.

The working conferences are structured differently. They are usually run by a working group and attendance is small and by invitation only. Their purpose is to create an atmosphere conducive to innovation and development. Refereeing is also rigorous and papers are subjected to extensive group discussion.

Publications arising from IFIP events vary. The papers presented at the IFIP World Computer Congress and at open conferences are published as conference proceedings, while the results of the working conferences are often published as collections of selected and edited papers.

Any national society whose primary activity is about information processing may apply to become a full member of IFIP, although full membership is restricted to one society per country. Full members are entitled to vote at the annual General Assembly, National societies preferring a less committed involvement may apply for associate or corresponding membership. Associate members enjoy the same benefits as full members, but without voting rights. Corresponding members are not represented in IFIP bodies. Affiliated membership is open to non-national societies, and individual and honorary membership schemes are also offered.

More information about this series at http://www.springer.com/series/6102

Matt Bishop · Natalia Miloslavskaya
Marianthi Theocharidou (Eds.)

Information Security Education Across the Curriculum

9th IFIP WG 11.8 World Conference, WISE9
Hamburg, Germany, May 26–28, 2015
Proceedings

 Springer

Editors
Matt Bishop
Department of Computer Science
University of California at Davis
Davis, CA
USA

Natalia Miloslavskaya
Moscow Engineering Physics Institute
National Research Nuclear University
Moscow
Russia

Marianthi Theocharidou
Institute for the Protection and the Security
  of the Citizen
European Commission - Joint Research
  Centre
Ispra
Italy

ISSN 1868-4238   ISSN 1868-422X   (electronic)
IFIP Advances in Information and Communication Technology
ISBN 978-3-319-18499-9   ISBN 978-3-319-18500-2   (eBook)
DOI 10.1007/978-3-319-18500-2

Library of Congress Control Number: 2015937375

Springer Cham Heidelberg New York Dordrecht London

Printed on acid-free paper

Springer International Publishing AG Switzerland is part of Springer Science+Business Media
(www.springer.com)

Preface

This volume contains the papers presented at the Ninth World Conference on Information Security Education (WISE9) held during May 26–28, 2015 in Hamburg, in conjunction with the IFIP International Information Security and Privacy Conference (IFIP SEC 2015). WISE9 is organized by the IFIP Working Group 11.8, which is an international group of people from academia, military, government and private organizations who volunteer their time and effort into increasing knowledge in the very broad field of information security education. WG11.8 has worked to increase Information Assurance Education and Awareness for almost two decades and this is the 9th conference of a successful series.

This year's conference received 20 submissions of high quality. Each submission was reviewed by at least 3, and on the average 3.3, Program Committee members. The committee decided to accept 11 full papers for publication. The acceptance rate of papers is 0.55. Two more invited papers from IFIP SEC 2015 were included in this volume due to their quality and high relevance to the WISE9 conference.

This conference took place due to the support and commitment of several individuals. First, we would like to thank all TC-11 members for giving us the opportunity to serve WISE9 and the working group. Our sincere appreciation goes to the members of the Program Committee, to the external reviewers, and to the authors, who trusted their intellectual work in our hands.

In particular, we would like to thank our colleague Prof. S.E. Goodman for proposing and chairing the panel on the theme of "Building National Cybersecurity Workforces," as well as our distinguished panel speakers for accepting our invitation and honoring the workshop with their presence and inspired discussions. We also thank the local organizers and hosts, first among them being the WISE9 Local and Logistics Chair Erik Moore. Last, but for sure not least, our appreciation goes to the WISE9 Conference Chair Lynn Futcher for her continuous and timely support.

Regarding the preparation of this volume, we would like to sincerely thank Erika Siebert-Cole and our publisher Springer for their assistance. Moreover, we would like to acknowledge the EasyChair conference management system, which was used both for managing the conference and creating this volume.

May 2015

Matt Bishop
Natalia Miloslavskaya
Marianthi Theocharidou

Organization

WISE9 is organized by the IFIP Working Group 11.8 – Information Security Education in conjunction with IFIP SEC 2015.

IFIP WG11.8 Officers

WISE9 Conference Chair

Lynn Futcher   Nelson Mandela Metropolitan University,
                South Africa

WISE9 Program Chair and Conference Secretariat

Matt Bishop   University of California at Davis, USA

WISE9 Program Chair

Natalia Miloslavskaya   National Research Nuclear University MEPhI,
                         Russia

WISE9 Publications Chair

Marianthi Theocharidou   European Commission, Joint Research Centre,
                          Italy

WISE9 Local and Logistics Chair

Erik Moore   Regis University, Colorado, USA

Program Committee

Matt Bishop	University of California at Davis, USA
Reinhardt Botha	Nelson Mandela Metropolitan University, South Africa
William Caelli	IISEC Pty Ltd, Australia
Nathan Clarke	University of Plymouth, UK
Melissa Dark	Purdue University, USA
Tamara Denning	University of Utah, USA
Ronald Dodge	United States Military Academy, USA
Lynette Drevin	North-West University, South Africa
Lynn Futcher	Nelson Mandela Metropolitan University, South Africa
Dimitris Gritzalis	Athens University of Economics and Business, Greece
Brian Hay	University of Alaska Fairbanks, USA
Hans Hedbom	Karlstad University, Sweden

Borka Jerman-Blazic	University of Ljubljana, Slovenia
Erland Jonsson	Chalmers University of Technology, Sweden
Suresh Kalathur	Boston University, USA
Sokratis Katsikas	University of Piraeus, Greece
Hennie Kruger	North-West University, South Africa
Costas Lambrinoudakis	University of Piraeus, Greece
Javier Lopez	University of Málaga, Spain
Leonardo Martucci	Karlstad University, Sweden
Vashek Matyas	Masaryk University, Czech Republic and Harvard University, USA
Natalia Miloslavskaya	National Research Nuclear University MEPhI, Russia
Erik Moore	Regis University, Colorado, USA
Kara Nance	University of Alaska Fairbanks, USA
Jacques Ophoff	University of Cape Town, South Africa
Ahmed Patel	National University of Malaysia, Malaysia
Sean Peisert	Lawrence Berkeley National Laboratory, USA and University of California at Davis, USA
Günther Pernul	Universität Regensburg, Germany
Reinhard Posch	IAIK, Graz University of Technology, Austria
Rayne Reid	Nelson Mandela Metropolitan University, South Africa
Carlos Rieder	Isec AG, Switzerland
Ingrid Schaumüller-Bichl	University of Applied Sciences Upper Austria, Austria
Corey Schou	Idaho State University, USA
Jill Slay	University of South Australia, Australia
Marianthi Theocharidou	European Commission, Joint Research Centre, Italy
Kerry-Lynn Thomson	Nelson Mandela Metropolitan University, South Africa
Alexander Tolstoy	National Research Nuclear University MEPhI, Russia
Johan van Niekerk	Nelson Mandela Metropolitan University, South Africa
Rossouw Von Solms	Nelson Mandela Metropolitan University, South Africa
Edgar Weippl	Vienna University of Technology, Austria
Stephen Wolthusen	Royal Holloway, University of London, UK
Louise Yngström	Stockholm University, Sweden and KTH, Sweden

Additional Reviewers

Leitold, Herbert	Nieto, Ana
Meier, Stefan	Stavrou, Vasilios

Building National Cybersecurity Workforces

Panel Abstract

S.E. Goodman

College of Computing and Sam Nunn School of International Affairs
Georgia Institute of Technology
Atlanta, GA 30332, USA
goodman@cc.gatech.edu

Issues of national cybersecurity workforces have become increasingly important as cybersecurity becomes a critical issue. This panel will explore several issues about cybersecurity workforces, including:

- How do we come up with need-based estimates of the size and make-up of national cyber security workforces?
- How would such workforces be characterized?
- What would be the balance between professionalization, functional duties, and relation to employing organizations and national needs?
- How might the answers to these questions differ across a range of nations?
- What might a broad spectrum of educational institutions do to stimulate supply and demand?

Contents

Syllabus Design

Innovative Methods

Realism in Teaching Cybersecurity Research: The Agile Research Process

Melissa Dark[1], Matt Bishop[2(✉)], Richard Linger[3], and Luanne Goldrich[4]

[1] Computer and Information Technology Department, Purdue University,
West Lafayette, IN 47907, USA
dark@purdue.edu
[2] Department of Computer Science, University of California, Davis,
Davis, CA 95616-8562, USA
mabishop@ucdavis.edu
[3] Cyber and Information Security Research Group, Oak Ridge National Laboratory,
Oak Ridge, TN 37831, USA
lingerr@ornl.gov
[4] Johns Hopkins University Applied Physics Laboratory,
Laurel, MD 20723, USA
Luanne.Goldrich@jhuapl.edu

Abstract. As global threats to information systems continue to increase, the value of effective cybersecurity research has never been greater. There is a pressing need to educate future researchers about the research process itself, which is increasingly unpredictable, multi-disciplinary, multi-organizational, and team-oriented. In addition, there is a growing demand for cybersecurity research that can produce fast, authoritative, and actionable results. In short, speed matters. Organizations conducting cyber defense can benefit from the knowledge and experience of the best minds in order to make effective decisions in difficult and fast moving situations. The Agile Research process is a new approach to provide such rapid, authoritative, applied research. It is designed to be fast, transparent, and iterative, with each iteration producing results that can be applied quickly. Purdue University is employing Agile Research as a teaching vehicle in an innovative, multi-university graduate program with government sponsor participation, as described in this paper. Because it simulates real-world operations and processes, this program is equipping students to become effective contributors to cybersecurity research.

1 A New Approach to Teaching Cybersecurity Research

Graduate programs in computer security emphasize research. Students who pursue a masters degree by writing a thesis or a doctoral degree by writing a dissertation are expected to do research that contributes to the body of knowledge. This dedicated study of a research problem requires students to be motivated and interested in the problem, and to understand the context in which the problem arises. The obvious way to do this is to study a particular facet of the problem in an applied circumstance. The student can then understand the constraints and

© IFIP International Federation for Information Processing 2015
M. Bishop et al. (Eds.): WISE9, IFIP AICT 453, pp. 3–14, 2015.
DOI: 10.1007/978-3-319-18500-2_1

available mechanisms, and attempt to develop a methodology or theory that will solve the problem in this specific instance. This leads to a good masters thesis. Doctoral students can then generalize the problem by relaxing the constraints and examining the broader problem in other contexts. This leads to a traditional research problem, and hence to the dissertation.

Unfortunately, graduate students are often not exposed to research until they begin their thesis or dissertation work. The goal of the work described in this paper is to provide this exposure by integrating research into the curriculum. Specifically, it focuses on obtaining applied research problems from sponsors, and having the students apply research processes to the problems under the guidance of both faculty and sponsors. This assures the results will be of interest to, and usable by, the sponsors. It also leads to broader, more traditional research work that stems from the application.

This work aims to enhance students' ability to plan, organize, and carry out research, especially as a member of a team, under the combined mentorship of faculty and sponsors. Additionally, it provides a basis for educational institutions to give students research opportunities that bridge theory to practice by focusing on real-world problems with real-world applications. It does so through the mechanism of a class on computer security research, run in conjunction with industry and government sponsors.

Because of the limited duration of the class, the students cannot complete a full, long-term research project. But they can begin or continue one, and so the research must be organized in a way that produces deliverables of some sort for the sponsor within the time constraints of the class. Further, the students must carry out and document their work in such a way that a completely different team of students can pick up where the original students left off, and continue the work. A new research methodology called *Agile Research* [5] provides an ideal way to do this.

This paper describes this work. The next section discusses the basis for the class, its organization, and how the work proceeds. Then we present a review of Agile Research, and follow up with a description of how the class implements the phases of that research methodology. We conclude with plans for the future.

2   Applied Research Class Organization

One of the focal activities of the INSuRE (Information Security Research and Education) project [1] is an applied research class. INSuRE is a consortium of 10 universities (Purdue University is the lead institution, and the other participants are Carnegie Mellon University, Dakota State University, Iowa State University, Mississippi State University, Northeastern University, Stevens Institute of Technology, the University of California Davis, the University of Maryland Baltimore County, and the University of Texas Dallas), plus the U. S. Department of Defense, Sandia National Laboratory, Pacific Northwest National Laboratory, Oak Ridge National Laboratory, the Indiana Office of Technology, and Hewlett-Packard. INSuRE aims to develop a partnership among sponsors that perform cybersecurity research and need the results to perform their missions, and cybersecurity researchers who conduct the research and produce results, including students and faculty at Centers of Academic Excellence in Information Assurance Research (CAE-R). INSuRE aims to become an agile, self-organizing, cooperative, multi-disciplinary, multi-institutional, and multi-level collaborative research project that can include both unclassified and classified research problems in cybersecurity. Currently, students from these 10 universities work on cybersecurity problems through coursework, directed independent study, and theses or dissertations.

The INSuRE applied research class provides an opportunity for students to work on problems provided by sponsors, as well as to be mentored by practitioners in the real world, rather than working solely on faculty-led research. More pressing and urgent problems are addressed, allowing the students to also benefit from the guidance of multiple and interdisciplinary research faculty from several institutions. The student-led research may in fact provide solutions for pressing national problems [7]. To facilitate scientific discovery, learning, and collaboration we use an open source software platform called HUBzero®. HUBzero includes a powerful content management system built to support scientific activities. Users on a hub can write blog entries and participate in discussion groups, but it is possible to do so much more. They can work together on projects, publish datasets and computational tools with Digital Object Identifiers (DOIs), and make these publications available for others to use not as dusty downloads, but as live, interactive digital resources. Simulation/modeling tools published on a hub can be accessed with the click of a button. They run on cloud computing resources, campus clusters, and other national high-performance computing (HPC) facilities and serve up compelling visualizations.

Prior to the class, faculty solicit research proposals from external organizations in government and industry. These proposals are a paragraph or two in length, and describe a research problem in fairly general terms. For example, a proposal to examine biometric systems of authentication might be as follows:

Title: Security of Biometric Authentication

Biometric devices provide information about people that is often used to authenticate their identity. This information must be associated with other data that is used to match up the data from the device to the user. This raises two questions. First, how easily can the biometric device be fooled into reporting incorrect measurements? And second, can the user change the comparison data on the system? This project explores the second question by determining how to change the comparison data for a given biometric device.

Sponsor: John Oldman

References:

- "Biometric Security", http://example.com/bio-security
- Jacob Marley, "Attacking a Biometric System," *Journal of Christmas Past* **3**(1) pp. 1–20 (Jan. 1951).

This Spring, the list includes projects on forensics, using code variation as a defense, an analysis of the proposed TCPcrypt protocol, machine-assisted semantic understanding of code, profiling industrial control system nodes, and the impact of known vulnerabilities upon layered solutions. The list is compiled and made available to faculty immediately and to students on the first day of the semester/quarter.

Obtaining sponsor interest has thus far been very successful; indeed, typically there are more proposed projects than there are students. Faculty members have solicited projects from people they know and, in many cases, have worked with. Most projects have come from government groups, but industrial firms and organizations have also proposed several. Interestingly, the latter typically take longer to prepare and get approval for projects than do the government organizations. For example, at least two companies were hoping to propose projects for the Spring term, but were unable to obtain the necessary approvals in time. Whether students can propose their own projects is up to the faculty member teaching the class. Some faculty allow this if the projects are substantial enough and deal with a current topic, on the basis that the students are best motivated when they are working on a project that they feel strongly enough about to propose. Other faculty members prefer that students select from the sponsor projects. As the proposed projects are typically broad, the students and sponsors have had no trouble narrowing down the projects to be of interest (sometimes enthusiastically so) to the students.

Complicating project selection is that different universities have different rules about working with sensitive projects. For example, the University of California at Davis does not allow any classified work to be done on campus, because that would restrict the ability of the researchers to publish (among other reasons). But other universities do. Proprietary work for industry has similar but different constraints. Thus, all sponsors must agree that, should the results and the work merit publication, the research from any project they propose can be published. As of now, this has not been a barrier to obtaining interesting projects.

The students prepare bids on at least two projects. First, the sponsors make a brief presentation to clarify their research needs and goals. Then the students engage in exercises to identify the knowledge, skills, and competencies required to work on the projects they are interested in. Each bid has four key components: a personal statement of interest, a description of the research problem (the most substantive section), the expected outcomes, and a description of student's skills, knowledge, and abilities relevant to the problem. Based on the students' bids, the faculty and research sponsors move quickly to form research teams.

Critical to the success of the project, of course, is that the team members work well together. In some cases, faculty and sponsors select the students that make up each team, which requires judging how amenable the members are to one another. The rationale for pairing students in teams can be based on student interest, expertise, and/or work style. In other cases, the students organize their own teams; the faculty and sponsor must accept the membership. Having students organize their own teams provides them with an opportunity to consider the factors that will constitute a research team, which is a valuable lesson. This ensures that the teams are balanced. Sometimes team membership changes after the initial formation. For example, at the University of California at Davis, a team of three members was reduced to two because one of the students became more interested in a different project, and so moved to the other team. However, all the students knew one another to some degree, and there were no problems with the change. The project has also started forming cross-institutional teams for the first time in Spring 2015. There is a three-person team with students from Purdue University and Mississippi State University, and another two-person team with a student from Dakota State University and one from Purdue University.

These teams next prepare a proposal, the contents of which are similar to that which would go into a National Science Foundation proposal (but with much less detail). The key components of the proposal are the review and analysis of previous work, and the statement of the specific aims of the project. The proposal also contains a schedule of milestones that the students believe they can meet, a plan describing how the students will approach solving the problem, and a bibliography. It also requires a realistic schedule and budget, a list of deliverables, and a discussion of any foreseeable difficulties and anticipated plans to overcome them. When writing the proposals, the students interact iteratively with sponsors and faculty to define the scope of the problem and near-term action steps to be taken. This step is critical in helping students assume the research problem as theirs as opposed to a work for hire, where the sponsors have "dictated" the scope of work and the students are simply following directions.

Once the proposal is approved, the students begin their research. As a first step, the students conduct a thorough literature review. This augments the quick literature reviews done earlier. Those reviews are simply aimed to show that the project has not been done earlier, and that it is substantial enough to advance the state of cybersecurity in some way. This literature review is structured around an argument or arguments. Typically, these arguments point out critical gaps in the existing literature, or how the work in that literature might be extended. If the goal of the research is to validate or correct a published result, the argument would explain the context of the work to be validated or corrected, why it is important, and what would happen if the prior results were incorrect or not corrected. The literature review is of sufficient importance that it is treated as an assignment and is weighted as much as the proposal is weighted.

Following that, the students begin acting on the plan laid out in the proposal. However, the teams are not left on their own to simply execute a 10-week project plan. Instead, teams meet every week with faculty and sponsors to report progress, the challenges encountered, how they are dealing with those challenges, and the next weeks goals. The goals sometimes change based on the challenges encountered. The rapid, successive iterations permit sponsors to modify incremental research goals and apply results based on intermediate findings as the work progresses (the principle of incremental management within a semester or quarter), and allows students to experience first hand the truly iterative and fast-paced nature of cybersecurity research.

The class requires students to prepare a midterm progress report that is delivered as a formal presentation to all classes across the universities via tele-conference, and a final project presentation that also includes a written report and poster. At the end of the semester, all students present the results of their research. For those on a semester system, this is a final presentation and report. For those on a quarter system, this occurs in the middle of the second quarter, and so is a penultimate presentation and report. Finally, those on the quarter system do a final project report and presentation at the end of the second quarter. The sponsor and the faculty member then evaluate the project.

One critical aspect of the final assignment is to document the progress made in a manner that allows the sponsor to iterate the next increment, and allows a team (at the same university or a different university) to pick the project up the next semester/quarter and continue the research, also in an agile, iterative manner. The specific manifestations of this differ based on the nature of the project. In some instances it includes a theoretical model that is sufficiently explained to allow a new team of student researchers to simulate and test the model. Another instance might be curating a dataset in a manner such that it is available for reuse and preservation. This type of documentation is essential to enabling the sponsor and faculty to incrementally manage research projects across semesters or quarters, and across institutions.

The sequence below summarizes the steps that the students follow [2]:

1. Project bid
2. Project proposal
3. Literature review
4. Progress report and presentation
5. Final report and presentation for schools on semester system; penultimate report and presentation for schools on quarter system
6. Final report and presentation for schools on quarter system.

Given that the class uses a non-traditional model of research, specifically one with a much tighter time-line than traditional research, a new model is needed. Fortunately, such a model has been developed: the Agile Research process.

3   Agile Research

Traditional, long-term research often involves extensive requirements definitions, comprehensive proposals, competitive awards, distributed organizational structures, complex funding protocols, and long-term performance that can extend for years. When the scope and scale of research requirements are large, these traditional processes and their management procedures are essential to maintaining control across collaborating organizations and reducing risks of overruns and non-performance. As such, they serve a vital role in conducting large-scale, long-term research projects to achieve national goals [3, 7].

But events occur in cybersecurity areas that require fast and decisive responses in order to protect national well-being and even survival [4]. These responses

would benefit from rapid and authoritative analysis by the best minds and organizations. The traditional research infrastructure was never intended for this
level of fast engagement and immediate application, and is not well suited for
these situations.

The Agile Research process [5, 6] was developed to address the need for fast
and effective researcher participation in situations where speed is an overarching
requirement. When attempts have been made to apply traditional methods in
these situations, the research results are often too late to be of use in the current
cybersecurity event, and wind up sitting on a shelf, unused and forgotten.

Agile Research is organized around sponsors, who pose research questions
to be answered, and researchers, who conduct the research and produce results.
Sponsors and researchers may be in the same or different organizations, and
may be organized in any number of ways provided the following principles are
satisfied [5, 6].

- *Predefined Infrastructure Principle:* Resources and logistics must be predefined and allocated before research needs emerge, to permit immediate deployment for fast engagement when needed. Agreements between sponsors and
  researchers regarding organizational roles, research capabilities, and contract-
  ing, funding, and intellectual property must be in place and ready to be
  instantiated in unforeseen circumstances with no delays. This "load-and-go"
  approach permits fast reaction by pre-positioned resources to unpredictable
  research needs unburdened by logistical constraints.
- *Incremental Research Principle:* Agile Research is structured into iterative,
  short-term, accumulating increments that each produces actionable results.
  Increments must first focus on understanding the problem, progress to solution
  strategies, and then to incremental solutions. Understanding how to organize
  research into a series of accumulating, referentially transparent increments
  requires careful planning. Early increments must provide a framework for
  inserting and composing later increments such that results accumulate with
  little or no revision of prior work.
- *Incremental Management Principle:* The incremental research process provides built-in, short-term checkpoints for sponsors to understand researcher
  progress, and to direct subsequent work based on incremental findings. Agile
  Research projects can be quickly refocused based on changes in both fast-
  paced problem environments and on intermediate shortfalls and windfalls
  in the research. Visibility, transparency, and clear communication between
  researchers and sponsors are essential for informed management decision-
  making.
- *Transferability Principle:* Agile Research projects may be carried out by one
  group of researchers, but ready transfer of results from one group to another
  must be possible if necessary. As research increments are completed and
  changes in direction are made, mechanisms for quickly repositioning the
  research and resources to a new team must be in place. This includes knowing
  where the research expertise exists for the next increment, as well as providing

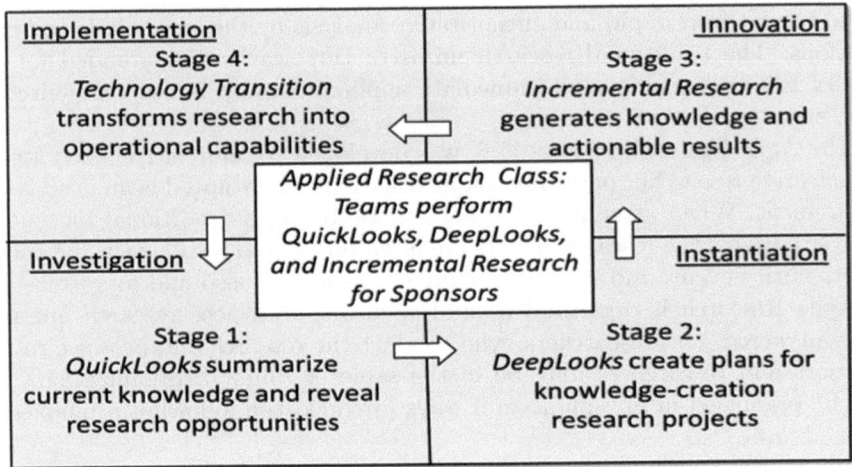

Fig. 1. The Agile Research process

supporting documentation that permits a new team to pick up the work seamlessly and rapidly.

Agile Research projects proceed through up to four stages, each culminating in researchers delivering results, either through briefings, white papers, tools, or a combination of these. At the completion of each stage, the sponsor decides whether and how to proceed. This process is summarized in Fig. 1.

- *QuickLook Stage:* This first stage generally takes days or weeks. It answers the question of what is known now about the problem. The research team clarifies research needs with the sponsor, explores the existing knowledge base, identifies subject-matter experts (SMEs), and provides recommendations to form a foundation for the research effort. This stage is deliberately made flexible to accommodate urgent or even emergency needs.
- *DeepLook Stage:* This second stage generally takes weeks. Based on results from the QuickLook stage, it answers the question of what the research can be expected to accomplish and how should it be done. It defines the research goals and plans in terms of iterative, accumulating increments that produce useful results for sponsors.
- *Incremental Research Stage:* This stage consists of multiple incremental steps, generally performed in weeks or months per increment. Each iteration adds to an evolving solution to the problem. This step-wise approach permits sponsors to modify incremental research goals and apply results based on the intermediate findings.
- *Technology Transition Stage:* Finally, if a project requires technology transfer, this stage, generally performed in months, provides specifications, prototypes, and support to guide technology implementation and operational use.

Agile Research is flexible. A project might require only a QuickLook to determine the state of knowledge for a particular problem. Or, a project could continue to a DeepLook to understand what the research could accomplish were it continued to the next stage, and how the research in that stage should be structured. The sponsor could then initiate the incremental research.

4   Putting the Class and Agile Research Together

The Agile Research model is well suited for the INSuRE class. Its structure corresponds closely to the first three phases of that model: the QuickLook Stage, the DeepLook Stage, and the Incremental Research Stage. Figure 2 depicts integration of the Agile Research process with the applied research class and the sponsoring organizations.

In the first stage of the class, the students do background work to prepare their bids and begin to scope the project. The sponsor starts the process by proposing a rather general research problem. Then each student makes a preliminary exploration of related work and decides on a view of the research project that he or she would like to explore. These recommendations will form a foundation for the research should the bid be accepted. In addition, the student identifies the competencies necessary by explaining why he or she is qualified to carry out the research.

This matches the QuickLook Stage of the Agile Research process almost exactly. The single difference is in the identification of the subject-matter experts. Rather than identifying others who are already these experts, the students explain why they should be considered, or will become, the subject-matter experts. In a non-class setting, the subject-matter experts may well not be the people performing the QuickLook stage. The timing also matches. The bidding

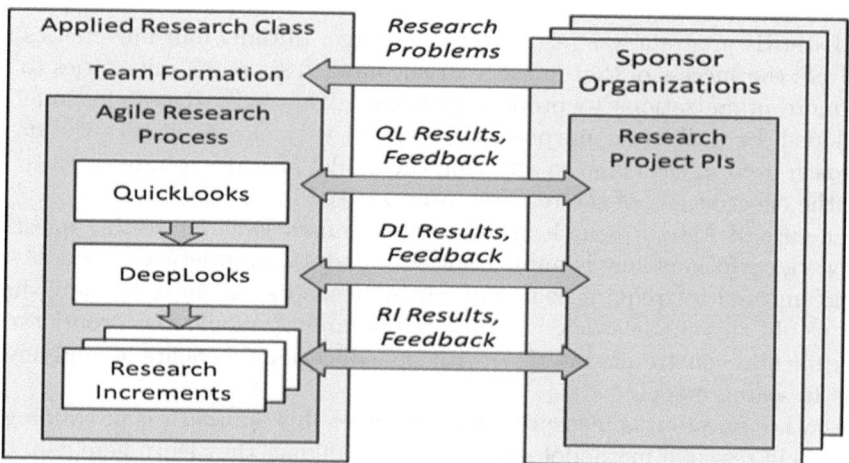

Fig. 2. Integration of Agile Research and applied research class

process for the class takes between 1 and 3 weeks; the controlling factor is the availability of the sponsors. In a non-class setting, the QuickLook would take about the same amount of time, again the availability of the sponsors being a critical factor.

The DeepLook Stage corresponds to the preparation of the proposal. Based on the bids, the students, faculty, and sponsors form the research teams. The teams then prepare proposals, as described above. The proposals present the goals of the research project, just as the DeepLook requires an answer to the question of what the research can be expected to accomplish. It contains a plan, saying how the research is to be done. Thus, it matches the DeepLook phase exactly.

The research itself instantiates the Incremental Research Stage of the Agile Research process. As noted above, the students meet with the sponsor weekly, with specific goals being set each week, and based on the results of each weeks progress, the sponsor can modify the research goals. Further, the sponsor can apply intermediate results from the teams work. This matches the goals and design of the Incremental Research Stage.

The design and implementation of the class reflects the principles of Agile Research. Of particular note is the transferability principle, which says that the results of one group must be transferable to another group. This is exactly how each team wraps up its results at the end of the class, because another team, possibly from another university or even split across multiple universities, may choose to pick up where the research was left off. Similarly, the incremental management principle requires that the research progress be incremental, with checkpoints for the sponsor and team to confer and determine how best to proceed; the sponsor will also receive actionable results at each increment. Again, this is reflected in the weekly meetings between the team and the sponsor.

5   Conclusion

The INSuRE program was begin over a year ago. Initially four universities were involved; the success of that initial year encouraged six more universities to join, and more organizations to propose problems. The Agile Research model was developed for a different purpose. However, it very closely mimics the desired approach used in the class, so applying the model provides a framework to support the effectiveness of the research process used in the class.

The use of Agile Research in this context raises some interesting questions. The work performed here is public (not classified nor proprietary), because some of the universities require that any research conducted must be publishable. How would this model work in a non-public arena? Would the proprietary or governmental constraints interfere with the educational benefits of applying the Agile Research model?

Another question is measuring how effective this approach is in training the students in research methodology. Can the techniques they learn here help them conduct the more traditional, long-term research needed for a doctoral dissertation? The intuitive answer is yes, because the structure of planning the research to produce publishable intermediate results will provide the students with a strong publication record when they complete their dissertation research, and the intermediate results may cause them to refocus the research if those results indicate the expected results will not hold or cannot be done. But the nature of the research—applied vs. pure—may pose a clash in the two approaches. Agile Research begins as a very applied research methodology, but traditional academic research is intended to extend the body of knowledge in ways that may not be immediately applicable. As an example, Riemannian geometry was developed in the 19th century as a demonstration that Euclid-s fifth postulate was in fact an axiom and not a provable proposition. It had no realistic applications until the 20th century, when the geometry of the universe was found to be Riemannian and not Euclidean. Were the goal of the research to develop a useful geometry, Riemannian geometry might never have been developed.

There is of course a place for both applied and pure research—indeed, pure research often provides the tools upon which applied research builds, and applied research often motivates the questions that guide pure research. Agile Research, with its emphasis on actionable results, is more applied, but leads to the fundamental questions that students can examine in their dissertations. Thus, it fills an important niche, and when used in an educational setting such as the INSuRE class described here, provides a firm foundation for students to begin a successful cybersecurity education and career.

Acknowledgements. Melissa Dark and Matt Bishop were supported by the National Science Foundation Grant Number DUE-1344369 to Purdue University, and by a subcontract from Purdue University to the University of California funded by that grant. Matt Bishop was also supported by the National Science Foundation Grant Number OCI-1246061 to the University of California at Davis. Any opinions, findings, and conclusions or recommendations expressed in this material are those of the author(s) and do not necessarily reflect the views of the National Science Foundation, Purdue University, or the University of California.

Richard Linger worked on this manuscript as an employee of UT-Battelle, LLC, under Contract No. DE-AC05-00OR22725 with the U.S. Department of Energy. The United States Government retains and the publisher, by accepting the article for publication, acknowledges that the United States Government retains a non-exclusive, paid-up, irrevocable, world-wide license to publish or reproduce the published form of this manuscript, or allow others to do so, for United States Government purposes. This submission was written by the author(s) acting in their own independent capacity and not on behalf of UT-Battelle, LLC, or its affiliates or successors.

References

1. INSuRE eager (2013). http://www.nsf.gov/awardsearch/showAward?AWD_ID= 1344369
2. Ecs 289m spring quarter 2015: Introduction to research in computer and information security (2015). http://nob.cs.ucdavis.edu/classes/ecs289m-2015-01/index.html

3. Branscomb, L.M., Auerswald, P.E.: Between invention and innovation an analysis of funding for early-stage technology development. Technical report NIST GCR 02–841, National Institute for Standards and Technology, Gaithersburg, MD, USA, Nov 2002. http://www.atp.nist.gov/eao/gcr02-841/contents.htm
4. Fonash, P., Schneck, P.: Cybersecurity: From months to milliseconds. IEEE Comput. **48**(1), 42–50 (2015)
5. Linger, R., Goldrich, L.: Agile research for cybersecurity. Technical report, Institute for Information Infrastructure Protection, Dartmouth College, Hanover, NH, USA, Jun 2014. http://www.thei3p.org/docs/research/agile08-2014.pdf
6. Linger, R., Goldrich, L., Bishop, M., Dark, M.: Agile research for cybersecurity: Creating authoritative, actionable knowledge when speed matters. In: Submitted for Publication (2015)
7. Maugham, D.: The need for a national cybersecurity research and development agenda. Commun. ACM **53**(2), 29–31 (2010)

Assurance Cases as a Didactic Tool for Information Security

Roberto Gallo[1,2]([⊠]) and Ricardo Dahab[1]

[1] University of Campinas, Campinas, SP, Brazil
{gallo,rdahab}@ic.unicamp.br
[2] KRYPTUS Information Security, Campinas, SP, Brazil
gallo@kryptus.com

Abstract. Secure systems are fiercely difficult to obtain - technical, procedural, human, and managerial aspects must be contemplated in a deep, yet holistic approach, which is a complex task even for experienced information security practitioners. Emerging information security "Assurance Cases" methodologies, such as the military NATO AEP-67, promise (time) effective practices for obtaining secure systems, making it a more reproducible process. In this paper we are the first to report the effectiveness of the Assurance Case methodology as a framework for teaching information security to both individuals and teams.

1 Introduction

In spite of over 30 years of research, new information security issues of every nature emerge in a growing rate. Indeed, achieving a secure system is arguably one of the most difficult tasks practitioners may face in their professional lives. Having a secure system demands a mix of procedural, technological, and scientific actions and capabilities that few teams have and even fewer professionals master.

Because of mainstream educational practice limitations, forming professionals that can handle both the comprehensiveness and depth necessary for success in information security is a challenge. These reasons are further explored ahead in this paper.

In this paper we report how Assurance Cases were successfully employed as the technical backbone of a course in secure system conception and implementation, as a means to achieve a holistic approach in teaching information security to both individuals and teams.

This paper is organized as follows: Sect. 2 presents related work, while Sect. 3 introduces the pedagogic model. In Sect. 4 the Information Assurance Case methodology is shortly introduced. The pedagogic model and the chosen assurance methodology form the course syllabus, presented in Sect. 5. The class experience and the experiment evaluation are reported in Sect. 6. Section 7 concludes and presents future work.

R. Gallo—Partially supported by Intel and Samsung research grants.
R. Dahab—Partially supported by CNPq grant 311530/2011-7, FAPESP Thematic Project 2013/25977-7, CAPES grant BEX 7046/14-6, and an Intel research grant.

2   Related Work

Education in information security has been receiving attention for over a decade [15,17]. In general terms, proposals can be classified with respect to four main aspects: duration, scope, integration with other curricula, and the existence of an underlying framework.

Because information assurance is such a broad subject and transversal to most IT-related major degrees, some authors consider that education in this area should start in the freshman year and continue throughout the student's formal education. It may even be possibly offered as a major degree itself [16].

Although ideal, however, this approach requires re-thinking entire curricula, demanding time, effort, faculty mobilization, and other resources. Thus, single courses, or workshop series are the prevailing approaches [13,14,18], as shown in a US survey [19].

When single, self-contained courses are considered, usually there is the need to compromise either in terms of scope or lab practice: as shown in [19], most security courses are in the form of lectures, even though hands-on classes were shown to present very promising results [11,12]. Also, it is important to note that the vast majority of hands-on single class courses are either on attacks, security management or risk assessment topics.

Our goal, however, is broader and builds upon the previous topics: the students, as teams, should become competent on *conceiving, designing, implementing, and evaluating* secure systems. Of course, such an agenda may be hindered by time constraints in a single term course and the inherent complexity of designing new systems.

To overcome these potential problems we adopted a double-edged approach: (a) in order to cope with the challenge of students designing new systems, we adapted a methodology for Electrical Engineering teaching based on product design [9,10], which provided a pedagogical framework for "students developing products"; and (b) in order to cope with time constraints, we took advantage of the Assurance Case Methodology's ability to factor work among students (see Sect. 4).

3   Pedagogic Model

Secure system conception, design and implementation is a complex task that requires creativity and deep and wide knowledge of theoretical and practical aspects. Thus, a traditional, purely narrative class, in the lines of what Freire called "The Banking Concept of Education" [1], is not the most appropriate for teaching these subjects. Although some concepts can and need to be explained to students, our hypothesis is that real knowledge on information security is better internalized by means of experiencing.

For that reason, we employed on our course the concepts of Jean Piaget's constructivism [2] and, more extensively, the theory of Experiential Learning by David Kolb [3] - where knowledge is gained by the appropriation and transformation of the students' experience. And because information security problems are seldom well structured and transversal to a broad range of areas, we were also inspired by Ivan Monsão's learn-by-doing teaching methodology [9,10], which precognizes that students must be given small yet real problems to work with, in a "close coaching" methodology, so that they may gain hands-on know-how (see Donald Schön [4] and John Dewey works [5]).

4   Assurance Cases - AC

We quote from NATO's Allied Engineering Publication #67 (AEP-67) [8]:

> System assurance is the justified confidence that the system functions as intended and is free of exploitable vulnerabilities, either intentionally or unintentionally designed or inserted as part of the system at any time during the life cycle. This ideal of no exploitable vulnerabilities is usually unachievable in practice, so *programmes*[1] must perform risk management to reduce the probability and impact of vulnerabilities to acceptable levels.
>
> The *Assurance Case* is the enabling mechanism to show that the system will meet its prioritized requirements[...] *It is a means to identify all the assurance claims, and from those claims (formally) trace through to their supporting arguments, and from those arguments to the supporting evidence.*

A key feature of ACs in general is that they support both quantitative and qualitative formal analysis of evaluation criteria, and then combines arguments in a logically structured way. ACs can be represented in different forms, depending on the objectives: graphs (readability), formal language (easy of processing), semi-formal (easy of writing, see Fig. 1). Assurance levels on claims can be presented as probabilities (calculated by logical-probabilistic methods) or simply by labels from risk analysis. We chose AEP-67 as our AC framework as it is both well-documented and a published standard.

A positive yet easy to overlook benefit of using assurance cases is the gained ability to factor both analytical and implementation work on a per component, per requisite (claim), per technology, or per life-cycle fashion, greatly reducing the need for "super-professionals" (with wide and deep knowledge). This is a key enabler of ACs as a methodological tool for education as we can focus on the team.

5   Course Syllabus

Once defined the technical and the educational methods we developed a syllabus where the (bold) objective was to teach students most security aspects of the conception, design and implementation of critical secure systems in a single-term

---

[1] A set of related measures or activities with a particular long-term aim: e.g. the British nuclear power programme.

- **CLAIM A**: "THE SOFTWARE IMPLEMENTATION ABIDES TO ITS SPECIFICATIONS", WITH **"medium assurance"**
    - "AND" **SUB-CLAIM-1**: "THE SOFTWARE BINARY CORRECTLY CORRESPONDS TO THE SOURCE CODE", WITH **"high assurance"**
        - ∗ **CONTEXT-1.1**: "ALL SOURCE CODE IS INTERPRETED AS ISO/IEC 9899:1999 STANDARD";
        - ∗ **ARGUMENT-1.1**: "THE SOURCE CODE IS COMPILED WITH A COMPILER THAT CORRECTLY TRANSLATES THE SOURCE CODE TO BINARIES" WITH **"high assurance"**
            - · **EVIDENCE-1.1**: "THE USED COMPILER IS COMPCERT, WHICH IS FORMALLY VERIFIED"
            - · **CRITERION**: "COMPILER WITH FORMAL VERIFICATION" FOR "HIGH ASSURANCE"
    - "AND" **SUB-CLAIM-2**: "THE SOURCE CODE ABIDES TO ITS SPECIFICATIONS", WITH **"high assurance"**
        - ∗ ...
    - ...
- **CLAIM B**: ...

Fig. 1. Text excerpt from an assurance case. Claim A is mid-level in terms of abstraction and can be a sub-claim of a number of higher-level claims, such as "the system provides only messages with origin authentication". Of course, in order to hold, Claim A also depends on a number of other factors (sub-claims), for example, to guarantee that the source code provided to the compiler is indeed the one intended by the programmer. As a result, the assurance level (or the probability of holding) for a claim with sub-claims is calculated by the composition of probabilities. A complete AC, even for small systems, can have hundreds of elements (claims, sub-claims, arguments, evidences, contexts, criteria, assumptions).

course (60 class hours over 4 months), so efficiency was a major concern. The course was offered both at graduate and undergraduate levels to computer and electrical engineer students and professionals. No specific prerequisites were set other than technical English proficiency.

The course started with 15 enrolled students and was organized in three parts: (A) introduction to security sub-areas, (B) project development, (C) attacks to others students' systems.

Grades were calculated from five main indicators: (i) project adherence to the security goals (claims) and functional requisites, (ii) related AC documentation quality and completeness, with special attention to quantitative and qualitative evidences and evaluation criteria; (iii) attack planning, execution and effectiveness; (iv) bonus questions and quests on selected topics (v) and a final written exam.

5.1   Part A - Introduction to Security Disciplines

This one month long part was basically a sequence of traditional lectures with two objectives: (A) to rise the overall security awareness level, and (B) introduce the Assurance Case Methodology. An important pedagogic objective was to move students away from Burch's [6] "unconscious incompetence" stage.

The program included: (i) security definitions, (ii) psychology and human factors, (iii) laws and standards, (iv) cryptography, (v) defensive programming, (vi) malwares and example attacks, (vii) side-channel attacks and hardware, (iix) discussion on a sample system, (ix) AEP-67 assurance case methodology.

5.2   Part B - Project Development

At the end of Part A, students were instructed to form two groups around projects. They were presented the option of proposing any non-trivial multi-user system of their choice (for which the teacher would establish security goals) or choose between two "messenger" projects, presented in Table 1, with a common general goal: to provide secure message functionality for a limited-size community of users.

Groups were formed and one leader per group was elected as point of contact and sole "trusted" element on their groups – the class instructor announced that he could covertly designate a team member (other than the leader) as a spy.

Table 1. Proposed project details

Title	"Spartan messenger"	"Athenian messenger"
Allowed limitations	Messages: text only, fixed-size, non-formatted, no history, no message delivery, No timing constraints	Text only messages, No timing constraints
Supporting assumptions	COTs semiconductors are free from targeted menaces, One member per team is trusted	Vanilla computing platform is free from targeted menaces (e.g. factory Android phone), One member per team is trusted, Adversary cannot act upon the hardware internals
Extras	Keep message history	Formatted messages, Voice messages
Security requirements (claims to support)	Data confidentiality, Meta-data confidentiality, Data integrity, Origin and data authentication	Data confidentiality, Meta-data confidentiality, Data integrity, Origin and data authentication, Plausible usage deniability, Replay attack protection
Threat model	Adversary has full power and can do anything other than the supporting assumptions, including deploying spies	Adversary has full power and can do anything other than the supporting assumptions, including deploying spies

This lead students to consider inside-threats from day one on their projects, resulting on a very rich security experience.

During two and half months, students were coached weekly (or twice a week upon request) and both projects and assurance cases were reviewed. Also, students formed e-mail groups for all internal project messages and included the instructor to promote further proximity with them. Technical hints were given whenever sticky points were identified either at live classes or on internal discussions on a close coaching but without direct coding or designing being performed by the instructor.

5.3   Part C - Attacks

Once finished, students provided their resulting project in its "product form" to the other team for security and functional evaluation. The sole provided documentation were user manuals and the security goals "claimed" by each group for their solutions.

Prior to the beginning of the 10-day attack phase, the class instructor introduced students on attack planning, attack surface and effort focus concepts so that they could make the most of their time. Also, instructor insisted in experimentation as a fundamental tool for success (and for learning).

At the end of the final phase, students had the opportunity to fix any security issues of their solutions prior to final grade evaluation.

5.4   Course Conclusion

The course was concluded with a single exam with the following motto: "when security is considered, more important than knowing a subject is the conscience of not knowing it". In Burch's terms, to be unconscious of one's own ignorance is much worse than any other learning phase when it comes to security, as even a single missing aspect is often fatal.

In that exam, although overall grades could range from 0 to 10, individual questions' grades ranged from -32 to $+16$: students were free to choose only the questions they fell comfortable with. This exam structure was carefully chosen so that penalization would not be counterproductive in pedagogic terms, while the nature of information security and related tasks were preserved.

6   Results

6.1   Project and Assurance Case Results

Both teams were able to finish their projects without considerable delays. They employed radically different techniques to achieve their goals with success, generating a handful of creative solutions.

A noteworthy and validating aspect was their ability to conclude, from the assurance case, industry best practices that naturally emerged during its compilation, such as (i) the benefits of the reduction of the trusted computing base, in a minimalistic approach (see Spartan messenger highlights bellow), (ii) the need for trusted designing tools (see compiler sub-claims on AC excerpt from Fig. 1), (iii) the importance of the supply chain (see Sect. 6.3).

Table 2 summarizes key group achievements and project features and highlights some characteristics.

Athenian Messenger

- **Stealth app launcher.** In order to sustain "plausible deniability" the team devised an app launcher scheme that presented no icons on the Android platform – the application was triggered when a user configurable specific phone number was dialed. The only app trace was a new running process at the device management screen;
- **Anti-permission leakage and interposition (Fig. 2).** The Android platform allows for a number of interposition mechanisms so that regular keyboards can be changed and even entire app screens can be precluded, representing a serious threat. The implemented solution was twofold: (i) when launched, an application scanned all device permissions looking for any hazardous interaction and warning the user if any was found; and (ii) the application was packaged with its own input method so that it was not threatened by rogue keyboards;
- **Dummy server.** Although a server was employed, its sole purpose was of message relaying. Even if the server were compromised, all authentication (data, origin) was performed by the devices themselves and no data breach would occur. To make this possible, a QR-code-based approach was implemented as a means for public-key exchange, when users were adding others to their contact lists;
- **Voice messages.** Groups implemented secure voice message functionality.

Spartan Messenger

- **Minimalistic approach.** Because trust on components should be accompanied by proper evidence, the group decided to have maximum control over their platforms: they acquired Raspberry Pi boards (Fig. 3) and stripped down a Linux distribution specifically for this project. All designed applications were minimalistic written in C language and any non essential feature was removed;
- **Private key protection.** Because private key protection was essential for data and origin authentication, private key was protected by multiple mechanisms, including full disk encryption. A good deal of creativity was employed when individual private keys were embedded on per-user binary application.
- **Assurance Case completeness.** The Spartan messenger team produced a very complete assurance case for their solution. Not only full lifecycle stages were considered, but also good security evidences were provided.
- **Resiliency.** The proposed solution did not rely on any servers, making it immune to some forms of DOS attacks. Because no scalability requirements were set, the group chose a broadcast/multicast network architecture allowing the implementation of strong metadata protection.

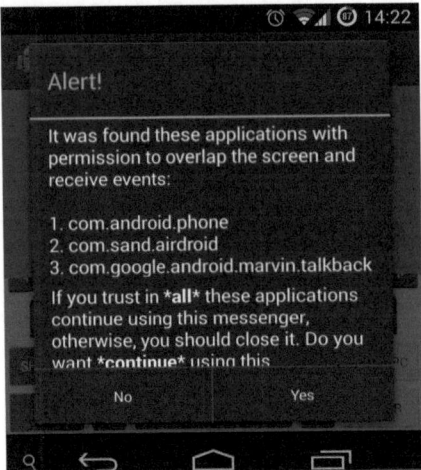

Fig. 2. Figure athenian permission scanner

Fig. 3. Figure spartan messenger hardware clients

Table 2. Key project and documentation results

Title	"Spartan messenger"	"Athenian messenger"
Chosen platform	Raspberry Pi + stripped Linux	Android phone
Architectural approach	Minimal trusted computing base	Security in layers
Cryptographic techniques for data in transit	Designed their own protocol using standard primitives. OpenSSL crypto library as core (SSL was not used)	Mixed their own protocol with Onion routing. GPG crypto core
Data at rest and binary protection	No user data at rest. Protected binaries by file system permissions and full disk encryption	SQCipher for database protection, with key derivation from user's PIN
Anti-metadata and side channel protection	Fixed size, fixed time package transmission with broadcast	Fixed size, fixed time package transmission with relay server
Highlights	Assurance case naturally showed strong security dependence over the supply chain. Very complete assurance case, split by lifecycle stage	Android permission scanning prior to application initialization, look for rogue apps. Innovative app launching scheme for plausible deniability

6.2   Attacks

Although only 10 days were given for attacking, teams deeply and consistently explored each others' solutions, giving rise to a number attack trials: 19 for Spartan team attacking Athenian app and 10 for Athenian team attacking Spartan solution.

Athenian Team on Spartan Solution. The attacks performed by the Athenian Messenger Team were distinguished by their systematization and the ability to find weaknesses (but not a violation) on the Spartan Messenger solution claims.

In terms of systematization, The Athenian Messenger Team organized potential attacks depending on: (a) attack surface, (b) active vs passive adversary model, (c) complexity, and (d) execution time. Of course, attack plans evolved while they learned more about the Spartan solution.

They performed analysis on network traffic, hardware I/O interfaces, the Linux image, and the application binaries, among others. They could find a sole marginal weakness - although no security claim was violated: on the Spartan solution, a user sends messages to other users using a command line application, passing message and receiver as arguments (e.g. ./sender receiver_name message). However, because the Spartan Team forgot to disable the BASH history, past messages persisted on the .bash_history file – this is only a moderate problem given that full disk encryption was in place.

The BASH history problem was solved for the final solution version.

Spartan Team on Athenian Solution. The Spartan Messenger Team spent considerable analytic and coding effort when attacking the Athenian Messenger. The first step was to decompile the application package (APK) so that further knowledge of the underlying cryptographic protocol was gained.

Although the protocol correctly addressed confidentiality, and data and origin authentication, it was susceptible to replay attacks. So, the decompiled code was used again, but this time to develop a Athenian malware that was able to perform replay attacks if the adversary could manage to be included as a contact into others' contact list. This was a violation of one of the intended security claims for the Athenian solution.

Interview with the Athenian team showed what Monsão calls "Aladdin Effect" as one of the root causes of the protocol defect: taking autentication mechanisms as black boxes instead of understanding their internals led to a deformed perception of its behaviour. Once students were presented to the precise mechanism functionality, they promptly corrected the protocol.

6.3   Student Perceived Evolution

In individual interviews, students reported that the Assurance Case methodology was an essential tool for systematizing protection mechanisms' coverage on their solutions.

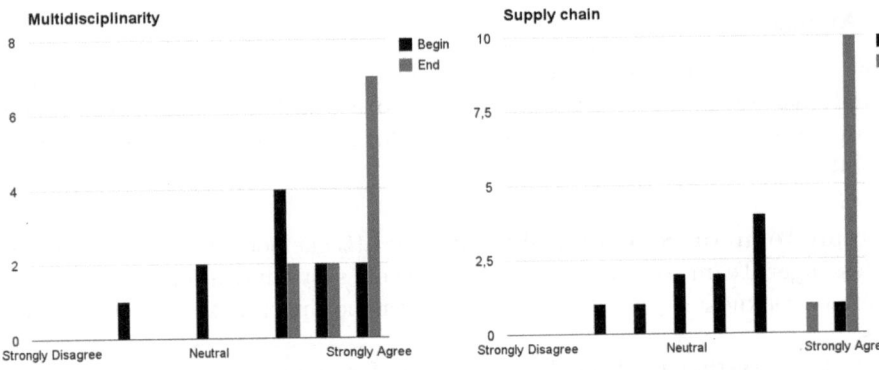

Fig. 4. Information security is a multi-disciplinary area

Fig. 5. The supply chain aspects are fundamental to information security

In order to proper capture student perception of their evolution, we conducted an anonymous and optional survey on their perception regarding seven relevant security aspects, comparing the perception they had at the beginning and at the end of the course. We used the Likert scale [7], with "1 for strong disagree", and "9 to strongly agree". Concordance with the following assertions were evaluated:

1. "Information security is a multidisciplinary area";
2. "Psychology [and social] aspects are fundamental to security";
3. "The supply chain aspects are fundamental to information security";
4. "Guaranteed security is a near impossible objective";
5. "Managerial methodologies are fundamental do security";
6. "Solution architecture is fundamental to security";
7. "Secure development methodologies are fundamental to security";

Figures 4 and 5 show the evolution for aspects 1 and 3 respectively, formatted as histograms. Although the number of samples is small, the course's influence is clear. Table 3 shows statistics for all seven assertions for the general group

Table 3. Statistics for assertion submitted to Likert-scale evaluation by students. Cell elements are organized in pairs: the first number is the average and second is the median.

Population	1	2	3	4	5	6	7
All begin	6.8-7	6.7-7	6.0-6	5.2-5	5.9-6	7.8-8	6.8-7
All end	8.5-9	8.5-9	8.9-9	7.5-8	8.5-9	8.6-9	8.4-9
Pro begin	7.6-7	7.6-8	6.2-7	5.6-6	5.4-6	8.2-8	6.0-7
Pro end	8.8-9	8.4-8	9.0-9	7.4-9	8.2-8	8.6-9	8.0-9

and a cut with only the students that work with security in a regular basis (professionals, with 4.8 year experience on average - 5 year median). There is no sensitive difference between the general group and the second group: both groups had seen similar improvements.

7   Conclusion

Although complex, learning how to conceive, design and implement secure systems can be achieved with a proper mix of baseline security awareness, coaching and managerial methodology. In this paper we reported the first (to the best of our knowledge) use of information assurance methodology as a backbone for security teaching. Both self-perception evaluations (with Likert scales) and practical results showed that students were able to internalize hands-on knowledge on the subject. Nevertheless, there is room for improvement - the attack phase was of intense learning, but its duration was reduced: the development phase took considerable time and closer schedule control would allow for smaller delays. Also, although course results are consistent, the sample size in terms of students is small.

Acknowledgement. We would like to thank our students for their dedication and the rich feedback they provided. We also like to thank Ivan Monsão for sharing his experience and feedback related to his pedagogic model.

References

1. Freire, P.: Pedagogia do Oprimido Paz e Terra, Rio de Janeiro (1970)
2. Mussen, P.H. (ed.): Piaget's Theory in Carmichael's Manual of Child Psychology, vol. 1. Wiley, New York
3. Kolb, D.A.: Experiential Learning: Experience as the Source of Learning and Development. Prentice-Hall, New Jersey (1984)
4. Schän, D.A.: The Reflective Practitioner: How Professionals Think In Action, Basic Books (1984). ISBN-10: 0465068782, ISBN-13: 978–0465068784
5. Archambault, R.D. (ed.): John Dewey on Education: Selected Writing. University of Chicago Press, Chicago (1974)
6. Adams, L.: Learning a new skill is easier said than done. http://www.gordon training.com
7. Likert, R.: A technique for the measurement of attitudes. Arch. Psychol. **22**, 5–55 (1932)
8. North Atlantic Treaty Organization - NATO: AEP-67 ENGINEERING FOR SYSTEM ASSURANCE IN NATO PROGRAMMES, February 2010
9. Monsão, I.: Uma Nova Metodologia de Ensino de Engenharia Elétrica Usando um Laboratório Paradidático, Ph.D. thesis, University of Campinas (2014)
10. Monsão, I.C., Dias, J.A.S., de Jesus F Cerqueira, J., da Costa, A.C.P.L.: A new methodology to teach electrical engineering using product development projects. In: 2012 IEEE Engineering Education: Innovative Practices and Future Trends (AICERA) (2012)

11. Sharma, S.K., Sefchek, J.: Teaching information systems security courses: A hands-on approach. Comput. Secur. J. **26**(4), 290–299 (2007). doi:10.1016/j.cose.2006.11.005. Elsevier

12. Wu, D., Fulmer, J., Johnson, S.: Teaching information security with virtual laboratories. In: Innovative Practices in Teaching Information Sciences and Technology, pp. 179–192. Springer International Publishing, Switzerland (2014). doi:10.1007/978-3-319-03656-4_16

13. Gandhi, R., Jones, C., Mahoney, W.: A freshman level course on information assurance: can it be done? here's how. ACM Inroads, ACM, September 2012. doi:10.1145/2339055.2339072

14. Logan, P.Y., Clarkson, A.: Teaching Students to Hack: Curriculum Issues in Information Security, SIGCSE Bull, ACM, February 2005. doi:10.1145/1047124.1047405

15. Maconachy, W.V., Schou, C.D., Ragsdale, D., Welch, D.: A model for information assurance: An integrated approach. In: Proceedings of the 2001 IEEE, Workshop on Information Assurance and Security. United States Military Academy, West Point, 5–6 June 2001

16. Howles, T., Romanowski, C., Mishra, S., Raj, R.K.: A holistic, modular approach to infuse cybersecurity into undergraduate computing degree programs. In: Annual Symposium On Information Assurance (ASIA), Albany, NY, 7–8 June 2011

17. Crowley, E.D.: Information system security curricula development. In: Proceedings of the 4th Conference on Information Technology Curriculum, CITC4 2003, ACM (2003). doi:10.1145/947121.947178

18. Pattinson, M.: CISA: COBIT: An ideal tool for teaching information security management. Inf. Syst. Control J. **6**, 33–36 (2004)

19. Manson, D.P., Curl, S.S., Torner, J.: A framework for improving information assurance education. Commun. IIMA: **9**(1), Article 6 (2009)

Cognitive Task Analysis Based Training for Cyber Situation Awareness

Zequn Huang[1], Chien-Chung Shen[1]([✉]), Sheetal Doshi[2],
Nimmi Thomas[2], and Ha Duong[2]

[1] Computer and Information Sciences, University of Delaware, Newark, USA
cshen@udel.edu
[2] Scalable Network Technologies, Inc., Culver City, USA

Abstract. Cyber attacks have been increasing significantly in both number and complexity, prompting the need for better training of cyber defense analysts. To conduct effective training for cyber situation awareness, it becomes essential to design realistic training scenarios. In this paper, we present a Cognitive Task Analysis based approach to address this training need. The technique of Cognitive Task Analysis is to capture and represent knowledge used by experts to perform complex tasks. Accurate characterization of cyber security experts' cognitive processes can be incorporated into training materials to teach novice cyber analysts how to think and act like experts. After performing Cognitive Task Analysis of cyber situation awareness, we identify the steps necessary for designing training scenarios and training workflows. In order to address the challenge of information overload confronting the cyber analysts, we identify and design attack-specific watch list items. During training, cyber analysts can tailor their own watch list items and triggering thresholds in order to detect cyber attacks faster. As the time it takes for cyber analysts to recognize, analyze, and respond to attacks is critical, we evaluate cyber analysts' performance based on their response time compared with the ideal attack timeline.

Keywords: Cognitive Task Analysis · Cyber situation awareness · Cyber situation awareness training scenario

1 Introduction

Cyber attacks, which refers to any computer-to-computer attacks that undermine the confidentiality, integrity, or availability of computer or information resident on it, have increased significantly in number and in complexity in recent years. Typically, a cyber attacker first exploits a system's vulnerabilities and infiltrates its network and/or hosts. Once the attacker gained entrance into the system, he may use it to monitor communications, steal critical data, discover new avenues of attack in related systems, take control of assets managed by the system or disable vulnerable networks, computers, and associated systems.

© IFIP International Federation for Information Processing 2015
M. Bishop et al. (Eds.): WISE9, IFIP AICT 453, pp. 27–40, 2015.
DOI: 10.1007/978-3-319-18500-2_3

Harmful outcomes of a successful attack include the attacker's ability to access sensitive data on the network and to control the hosts and network resources.

Situation awareness involves perception of evolving status and attributes of elements, comprehension of combined observations to evaluate the current situation in order to make predictions of possible future outcomes based on past experience and knowledge. Specifically, situation awareness in the cyberspace (Cyber Situation Awareness [1,2], or CSA for short) is an immensely cognitive task which is embedded in a large multi-layered sociotechnical system of cyber analysts, computers, and networks. In CSA, cyber analysts have to collect data and seek cues that form attack tracks, estimate impact of observed attack tracks, and anticipate moves (actions, targets, time) of attackers. Presently, effective performance in CSA is hampered by the enormous size and complexity of the network, by the adaptive nature of intelligent adversaries, by the high number of false alarms generated by intrusion detection systems, by the lack of ground truth to assess defense performance, by organizational stove-pipes thwarting collaboration, and by technologies that lack an adequate understanding of the human needs.

In particular, in contrast to environments that are bounded by physical constraints and/or geographical features, cyberspace possesses the following unique features which further impose extraordinary cognitive challenges on cyber analysts [3]. First, while a cyber analyst is fully aware of the boundaries of his/her managed networks, the external cyberspace is boundless with minimal geographical features. As a result, the environment from which a cyber analyst has to perceive salient cues is vastly larger and more difficult to comprehend. Comprehending even a small segment of cyberspace is challenging. Second, the speed at which the cyberspace changes is much faster, where new vulnerabilities and their corresponding exploits are continuously emerging, and new offensive technologies are constantly being developed. Furthermore, modern exploits are either employed via misdirection (e.g., a DDoS attack is conducted by a Botnet of compromised computers) or delivered passively via embedded malware. Third, everything a cyber analyst knows about the environment is a virtual representation of the cyberspace in terms of digital information (e.g., intrusion alerts and firewall logs). In addition, the cyber analyst only sees the information that his/her (software) sensors are capable of detecting in a form that can be rendered on monitor screen. Because perception and comprehension of cyberspace is inherently constrained by technology artifacts, cyber analysts' ability to develop situation awareness is greatly limited by the degree to which the network's sensors are correctly configured and capturing data.

Furthermore, cyber analysts are faced with extraordinary amounts of information (such as various IDS and audit logs) to sift through, and CSA demands that various pieces of information be connected in both space and time. This connection necessitates team collaboration among cyber analysts working at different levels and on different parts of the system. It is anticipated that team CSA can be carried out to systematize information coordination and team collaboration for CSA effectiveness and resilience. As cyber attacks are becoming more frequent and more complex, the need for more effective training of cyber analysts and their collaborative efforts to protect critical assets and ensure system security is also elevated.

Cognitive Task Analysis (CTA [4]) is the extension of traditional task analysis techniques to yield information about the knowledge, thought processes and goal structures that underlie observable task performance. The outcome of CTA describes the performance objectives, equipment, conceptual knowledge, procedural knowledge and performance standards used by experts as they perform a task. Accurate identification of cyber security experts' cognitive processes can be adapted into training materials to teach novices how to perform like experts. In this paper, we present a solution for cyber training which uses a CTA based approach to gain insight into the cognitive demands and workflow of cyber analysts and design cyber security training scenario and training workflow. Then, we evaluate cyber analysts' performance based on their response time of detecting cyber attacks comparing with estimated attack ideal timeline.

The remainder of the paper is organized as follows: Sect. 2 describes related work and background. Section 3 introduces the Cyber security training and assessment framework infrastructure. In Sect. 4, we identified the steps necessary for designing cyber security training scenarios and training workflow after performing Cognitive Task Analysis. Section 5 describes two cyber security training scenarios. The scoring algorithm to evaluate the performance of cyber defense analysts is presented in Sect. 6. To evaluate the usability of the training system, Sect. 7 presents the questionnaire that cyber analysts are asked to answer in order to evaluate the cognitive validity of training. Finally, Sect. 8 concludes the paper.

2   Related Work and Background

General reviews of current simulation-based cyber security training systems are given in [5]. CyberCog [6] is a synthetic task environment for understanding and measuring individual and team situation awareness, and for evaluating algorithms and visualization intended to improve cyber situation awareness. CyberCog provides an interactive environment for conducting human-in-the-loop experiment in which the participants of the experiment perform the tasks of a cyber analyst in response to a cyber attack scenario. CyberCog generates performance measures and interaction logs for measuring individual and team performance. CyberCog has been used to evaluate team-based situation awareness. CyberCog utilizes a collection of known cyber defense incidents and analysis data to build a synthetic task environment. Alerts and cues are generated based on emulation of real-world analyst knowledge. From the mix of alerts and cues, trainees will react to identify threats (and vulnerabilities) individually or as a team. The identification of attacks are based on knowledge about the attack alert patterns.

Designed for better understanding of the human in a cyber-analysis task, idsNETS [7], built upon the NeoCITIES Experimental Task Simulator (NETS), is a human-in-the-loop platform to study situation awareness for intrusion detection analysts. Similar to CyberCog, NETS is also a synthetic task environment. The realistic scenarios are compressed and written into scaled world definitions

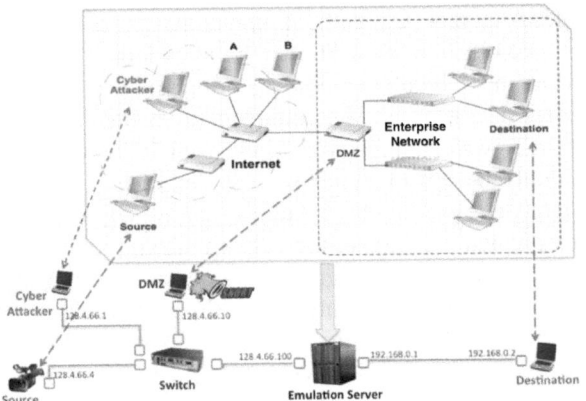

Fig. 1. Usage example of Live-Virtual-Constructive (LVC) framework

and the simulation engine is capable of interpreting the scaled world definitions into a simulated environment, running the simulation, and responding to user interaction. In [7], several human subjects experiments have been performed using the NETS simulation engine, to explore human cognition in simulated cyber-security environments. The study indicates that the teams who had more similar skill sets displayed a more cohesive collaboration via frequent communication and information sharing.

The main difference between CyberCog/IdsNETS and LVC framework (Live-Virtual-Constructive [8]) is that while CyberCog and IdsNETS are synthetic task environments, the LVC framework is an actual simulator/emulator. A synthetic task environment may rely on previous incidents to generate the sequence of alerts and cues corresponding to those incidents, The LVC framework is able to simulate previous incidents as well as generate new simulated or emulated incidents on the fly. The LVC framework supports a hybrid network of actual and virtual machines so that attacks can be launched from an actual or a virtual host, targeting an actual or a virtual host. Figure 1 illustrate the usage examples of the LVC framework that combines physical machines and virtual network environment to perform cyber attacks and defense.

3   Cyber Situation Awareness Training and Assessment Framework Infrastructure

The system infrastructure for the proposed Cyber Situation Awareness training and assessment framework is shown in Fig. 2. As shown in the figure, lesson database contains different kinds of cyber attack scenarios with different difficulty levels. We apply Cognitive Task Analysis on a set of tasks and use the information to generate scenarios for training purposes. For each task, we identify major events and watch list items needed for decision making. The trainees are able to tailor their watch list and triggering threshold conditions.

With the proceeding of training scenario, data such as IDS log, network flow, and trainee specified trigger alerts will be reported to the trainee. After analyzing these data, the trainee should think whether it is an attack or false alarm based on prior knowledge and decide the type of attack through attack model matching. Interactions and team discussions can be conducted through the Shared Events Viewer and team communication module. If the team members still cannot achieve agreement, the fuzzy logic based team consensus decision making module can help chose the most acceptable solution for the entire team.

The assessment metrics will include trainee response time with respect to critical cues and evaluate the actions taken or decisions made to determine potential attacks. By comparing trainees' response time and estimated attack ground truth timeline, we can identify if the response is fast or slow. The performance evaluation module can provide performance score and feedback to trainees, as well as adjust the next training lesson's difficulty level based on trainees' performance. Furthermore, Situation Awareness Global Assessment Technique (SAGAT) is used to get feedback from trainees in order to evaluate training system usability and effectiveness.

4   Cyber Situation Awareness Training Scenarios Design

We propose realistic training scenarios for Cyber Situation Awareness training and assessment based on the LVC framework, which enables cyber analysts to experience cyber attacks and to learn how to detect ongoing cyber attacks. Designing cyber security lessons to involve cyber analysts in activate learning requires careful planning. Cognitive Task Analysis technique [9] is a prominent approach that captures knowledge representation used by experts to perform complex tasks. We utilized a combination of three knowledge capture techniques: observing cyber security competitions, examining critical incidents, and reviewing relevant papers of structured interviews with cyber security experts and information assurance analysts [10]. We elicit the knowledge about how, when, where, and why when performing cyber defense task. This knowledge can be applied into design consideration for cyber security training scenarios.

Notice that human cyber analysts have to check thousands of events each day from many sources such as system logs, configurations, traffic logs, IDS log, and audit logs in order to determine whether there are real attacks or false positives; therefore, they would be soon overwhelmed by tremendous data and forced to ignore potentially significant evidences introducing errors in the detection process. In order to solve the tremendous cognitive demand faced by cyber analysts, we identify and design watch list items relating to cyber attacks. Cyber analysts can tailor their own watch list items and triggering thresholds in order to detect cyber attacks faster.

Six steps necessary for building training lessons are as follows:

1. Previous related work review
2. Training objective definition
3. Training scenario creation

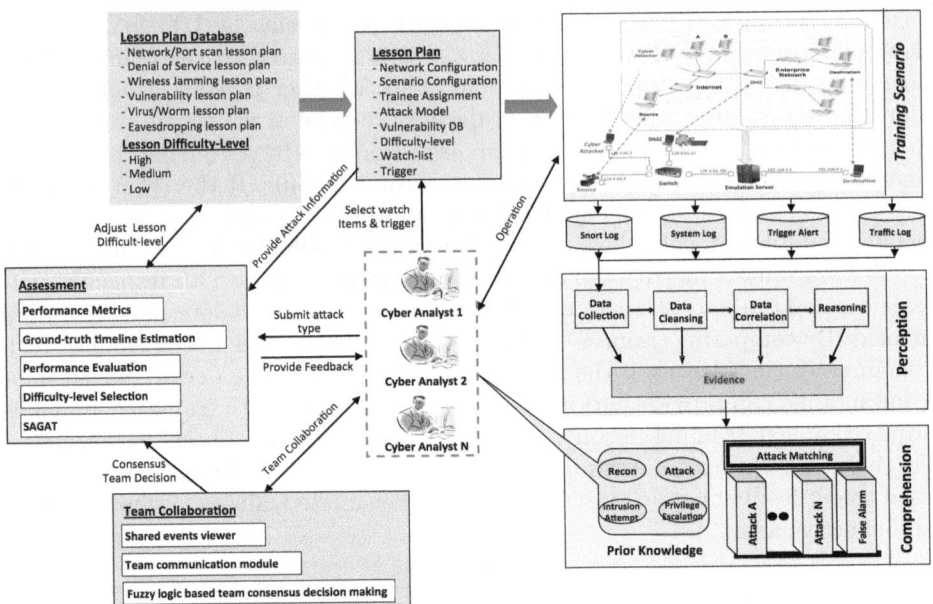

Fig. 2. CSA training and assessment system infrastructure

4. Cyber analyst watch-list definition
5. Cyber analyst response recording
6. Performance assessment

Based on the design steps, the training workflow is shown in Fig. 3, which contains the following steps:

Step 1: Instructor creates a training scenario for the cyber security training that includes a cheat sheet for the cyber attack/defense aspect based on the lesson objective. The Cheat Sheet includes the watch list items critical to the cyber attack and the attack ideal timeline denoting the attack start and success time. Cyber analyst should react to the cyber events in simulation and perform certain actions that demonstrate his/her understanding of cyber attacks.

Step 2: Instructor sets up training scenario with the tool providing the widgets to enable the instructor to enter in the information from the cheat sheet.

Step 3: When training scenario begins, the specified trigger alert and other log data specified by cyber analyst will be sent to cyber analyst side. After analyzing these data, cyber analyst should think whether it is an attack or false alarm based on prior knowledge and decide the type of attack through attack model matching.

Step 4: During the training, with cyber analyst's actions being logged continuously, the training system can determine whether the response actions of cyber analyst are following the ideal timeline enumerated by instructor in the cheat sheet.

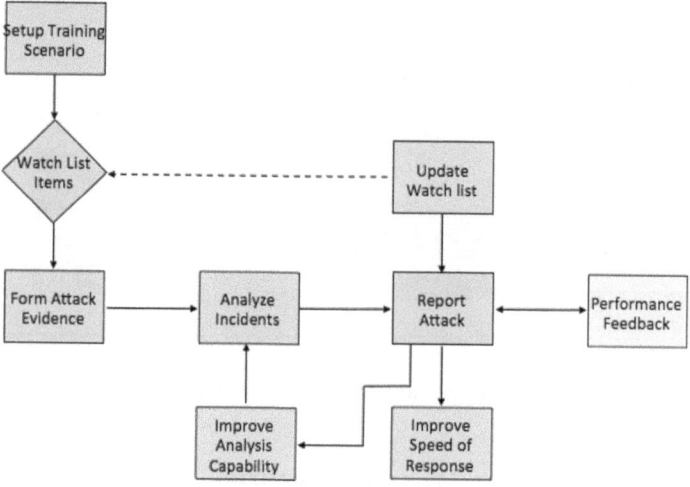

Fig. 3. Workflow for training system

Step 5: Based on cyber analyst's response and the ideal timeline, the score for cyber analyst will be computed using devised scoring mechanisms, and provided to cyber analyst as part of after action review.

Step 6: After obtaining performance assessment report, cyber analysts should think about selecting different watch list items or improving analysis capability for the next lesson.

Based on the tailored lesson scenario, cyber analyst will learn the knowledge required to monitor network conditions and identify ongoing attacks. After completing the cyber security training, cyber analysts will be able to do the following with respect to a given set of known attacks:

– List the relevant parameters to monitor and know the characteristics of these parameters under normal and abnormal operations.
– Recognize symptoms of network attacks. Specifically, cyber analyst will be able to isolate common characteristics of network under attack and be able to distinguish the characteristics that are particular to each attack.
– Given a particular set of current conditions (monitored parameters), be able to analyze what kind of attack is occurring and how the attack was launched.
– Demonstrate proper procedure of remedial actions, including selection of countermeasures to apply and where in the network to apply them.

5   Cyber Situation Awareness Training Scenarios

Guided by the lesson design steps and goals of cyber security training, we propose port/network scan and denial of service cyber security training scenarios for the Cyber Situation Awareness training and assessment system.

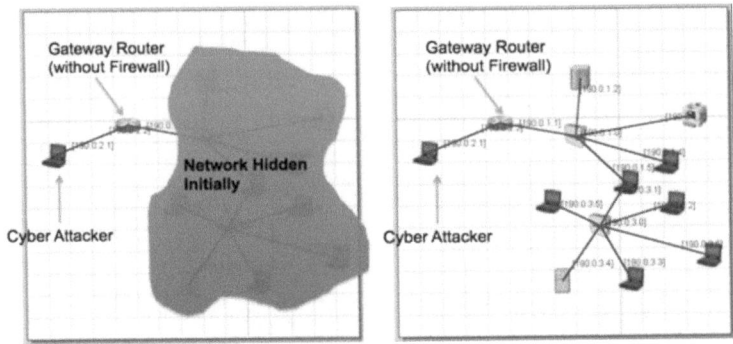

Fig. 4. Port/network scan lesson scenario

5.1   Port/Network Scan Training Scenario

Usually an attacker first attempts to obtain information concerning a network in order to choose the following malicious actions. Specifically, after network scan, an attacker is able to discover the number of hosts, the IP addresses and the network topology. The next step an attacker may take is to perform a port scan [11] to discover which hosts are critical and what services are running on the various hosts. The obtained information can be used by an attacker to plan attack attempts targeting various vulnerabilities.

An example of lesson scenario on how to perform network and port scan is illustrated in Fig. 4. Initially, the core gateway router is configured without firewall. Before performing a network scan, the "inside" network is not visible to the outside world. The attacker then attempts to obtain information on the internal network by launching a network scan. Without firewall protection at the router, the network scan is able to discover the number of hosts, IP addresses and the network topology by sending a bunch of probe packets. Once an attacker learns the IP addresses of hosts and network connectivity, he/she can launch port scan to discover applications such as web server, FTP server running on the hosts and other devices connected to the hosts.

For the purpose of facilitating cyber analysts' analysis, we define network scan as a procedure for identifying active hosts on a network. After observing the network traffic that contains certain numbers of distinct probes within a short period of time from a single anomalous source, it might be a potential network scan attack. The port scan is defined as an attack that sends requests to a range of server port addresses on a host with the goal of finding open ports and corresponding services running on the ports. By observing several requests to a range of port addresses, it might be a potential port scan attack.

5.2   Denial of Service Training Scenario

Denial of Service (DoS [12]) attacks aim at stopping the target system from working properly through recruiting a large number of "zombie" machines to send high volumes of ordinary traffic. The DoS lesson objective is to train cyber analysts to understand DoS attacks and their detection methods. In this lesson, we will study three types of DoS attacks:

- Basic DoS attack: the attackers send large volume of UDP traffic to the victim host or network. Such traffic consumes network bandwidth, buffer memory as well as CPU resources.
- TCP SYN DoS attack: the attackers send TCP SYN packets to the victim host. Each TCP SYN packet opens a new TCP connection at the victim computer; thus, consuming transport-layer resource.
- IP Fragmentation DoS attack: the attackers send partially fragmented IP packets to the victim host. The victim computer buffers these fragmented packets and wait for remaining segments.

To identify DoS attacks, cyber analysts first need to differentiate attacks from normal bursts of network requests in order to reduce the rate of false alarms. Therefore, we need to compare burst requests with behavior of normal requests. In general, requests from DoS attacks share the same target, such as tens of thousands requests are trying to access a specific address. Once cyber analysts identify the incoming requests are indeed DoS attacks, the next information cyber analysts need to acquire is what kind of DoS attack it is and what attack techniques it is employing. Since cyber analysts already know about the details of the requests from the system logs, cyber analysts can determine the type of DoS attacks and then take corresponding defending actions.

As introduced previously, cyber analysts should consider three DoS attack scenarios: basic DoS attack, TCP SYN DoS attack, and IP Fragmentation DoS attack. Basic DoS attacks involve sending a large volume of traffic to the host, exhausting the host's processing and memory resources and making unable to serve more normal traffic. As a result of sharp increasing in the size of memory and CPU usage of server hosts. TCP SYN attack happens when attackers send a flood of TCP/SYN packets with faked sender addresses. Each packet is treated as a connection request and the server maintains a half-open connection for each request. The server send TCP/SYN ACK packets back to the faked senders and waits for the responses. Since the sender addresses are faked, the responses will never come. And the number of half-open connections quickly saturate the buffer resources of the server, rendering it unable to serve future legitimate requests. Another technique of DoS attack is via IP fragmentation. Observing larger IP fragments in the IP buffer indicate the potential IP Fragmentation DoS attack.

Figure 5 shows an example DoS exercise scenario, which includes nine "zombie" machines that can send high volumes of ordinary traffic to the target victim machine. An attack targeting at the HTTP server typically involves sending a large number of requests, each of which consumes significant resources. This then limits the ability of the server to respond to requests from other users. Besides, HTTP requests may make database queries. When costly queries are constructed, a large number of requests could severely overload the server and limit its ability to respond to legitimate requests. The attackers can start either

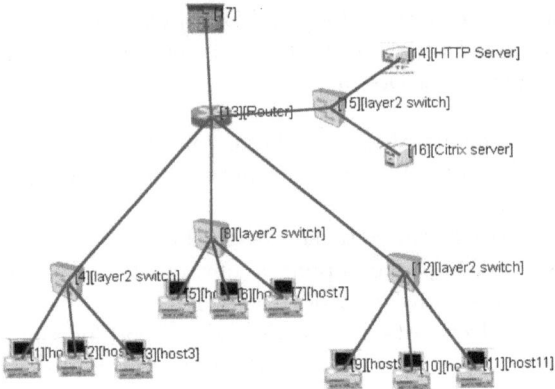

Fig. 5. DoS lesson scenario

one of the three types of DoS attacks. The magnitude and difficulty level of the exercise scenario can be controlled by the number of "zombie" machines as well as traffic volume.

To perform DoS attack detection, traffic flow monitoring is the key. Example watch list items about system information and traffic flow include CPU and memory resource usage, number of incoming flows, and aggregated traffic rate as shown in Table 1.

6   Performance Metrics and Scoring Algorithms

To monitor the activities of and provide feedback to a cyber analyst during training sessions, we adapt the method of *timeline analysis* for performance assessment. The ideal timeline of a training exercise is gauged based on the specific attack scenario and its configuration. After a training exercise starts, all of an cyber analyst's actions are continuously logged so that the training system can determine whether actions taken by the cyber analyst follow the ideal timeline and match the expected activities. This evaluation can be provided as feedback to the cyber analyst during training. For instance, if a cyber analyst fails to identify attacks in time, the system can proactively provide hints to the analyst, or share the views of other cyber analysts. A cyber analyst may also ask for hints from the instructor. The performance of a cyber analyst is evaluated based on the response time of correctly identifying specific cyber attacks.

Figure 6 depicts how the measurement of memory usage can be used to characterize the ideal timeline for a DoS attack. The time period is divided by two memory usage thresholds into three phases: before attack, during attack, and after successful DoS attack. Based on the pre-defined memory usage thresholds and the DoS training lesson's configuration (such as the number of packets to be sent, the frequency of sending packets, the start and end times), a DoS attack's start time and its time of successful attack can be determined. Similarly,

Table 1. DoS exercise watching list

CPU utilization	CPU utilization is calculated by CPU load as a percentage of the CPU capacity
Memory usage	Memory consumed during certain period
Network traffic	- Network-FIFO, Total packets queued
	- Network-FIFO, Average queue length
	- Network-FIFO, Longest time in queue
	- IP, Number of IP Fragments received
	- IP, Number of IP Fragments dropped
	- IP, Buffer Size
	- UDP, Number of packets received
	- UDP, Number of bytes received
	- TCP, Number of packets received
	- TCP, Number of bytes received
	- TCP, Number of SYN packets received
	- TCP, Number of SYN ACK packets sent

the method can be applied to other DoS metrics such as CPU usage, number of incoming flows, and aggregated traffic rate to generate their corresponding timelines. By combining these timelines together, an ideal timeline for the DoS attack can be generated.

Based on the response of cyber analysts and the ideal timeline, scores for the performance of cyber analysts can be computed using the devised scoring mechanisms, and provided to the cyber analysts as one component of their after action review. By comparing cyber analysts' response time against the ideal timeline, we can determine whether a cyber analyst responds in a timely manner. For instance in Fig. 6, assuming a DoS attack starts at time 10 s and sustains for 35 s, and the victim host shuts down at time 45 s due to DoS attack, cyber analyst has a time window of 35 s to identify the ongoing DoS attack. If cyber analyst identifies this DoS attack at time 20 s, cyber analyst's response is considered fast

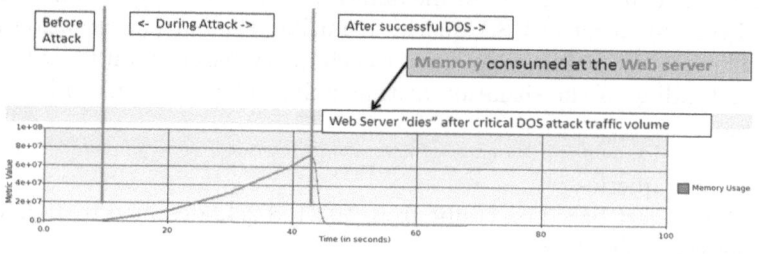

Fig. 6. Use memory usage metric to gauge ideal timeline for a DoS attack

enough to score a higher point. In contrast, if cyber analyst does not identify the DoS attack until the victim host shuts down, no point will be given.

To evaluate the performance of cyber analysts, a set of performance metrics has been adopted:

- Lesson magnitude and difficulty levels (W_D): stands for the severity of attacks or the difficulty level of achieving an attack goal. A scenario's difficulty level is specified in one of three categories: high, medium, or low.
- Response time (W_T): measures cyber analysts' responsiveness to correctly recognizing cyber attacks.
- Correct detection of attacks (W_C): identifies the existence of a real attack and its type.
- Damage impact (W_I): measures attacks' impact on victim's confidentiality, integrity, and/or availability.

Based on the performance metrics, the performance score of cyber analysts can be calculated by the following formula:

$$Score = W_D * (\sum_{k \in \{T,C,I\}} W_k * K_k)$$

where $K_k, k \in \{T, C, I\}$ is the weight factor for each performance metric. Notice that the lesson difficulty level W_D is separated from other performance metric during score calculation. This is because the more difficult of the lesson, the higher score is given since cyber analysts have to spent more time and effort to perform the defense task. For the purpose of consistent computation, each weight factor is normalized to the value between 0 and 1. Take difficulty level W_D as an example, training lesson labeled with "Low" difficulty has weight factor value 0.4 and "Medium" difficulty training lesson is given weight value 0.7.

7   Evaluate Cognitive Validity of Training

In order to evaluate the usability of the training system and the effectiveness of training, Situation Awareness Global Assessment Technique (SAGAT [13]) is used. SAGAT covers the three levels of CSA including Level 1 (perception of data), Level 2 (comprehension of meaning), and Level 3(projection of the near future). Typically, a set of CSA queries regarding the current situation is asked and participants are required to answer each query based upon their knowledge and understanding of the situation at that point. The questions to be asked are as follows:

1. CSA related queries
    (a) An IDS alert based on traffic from 192.168.2.42 destined to 192.168.1.252 is best classified as?
    (b) Which watch list item is abnormal?
    (c) Is it an attack or false alarm?

    (d) What is the impact for the current attack? Any confidentiality, integrity, or availability loss?

    (e) What actions should be performed to stop this attack?

2. Participant satisfaction

    (a) Is the training tool easy to use?

    (b) Is the information displayed in a way that is easy to comprehend?

    (c) Does the tool provide information needed to achieve lesson goals?

    (d) Are the lesson contents at the appropriate difficulty level for the cyber analysts?

    (e) Are the hints useful?

3. Knowledge acquisition

    (a) Does the cyber analysts grasp the main objectives of the lesson?

    (b) Does the lesson learned lead to intended decision-making skills?

4. Behavior changes

    (a) How does the acquired knowledge affect the cyber analysts in future operations?

    (b) Will the cyber analysts be able to detect and identify DoS attacks faster?

8   Conclusion and Future Work

Accurate characterization of cyber security experts' cognitive processes can be adapted into training materials. In this paper, we described two cyber security training scenarios: port/network scanning and denial of service after performing Cognitive Task Analysis. We also defined the metrics for performance evaluation and the corresponding scoring algorithm. For a comprehensive CSA training system, it is more than just an abstract notion of how well people respond to attacks, but also, evaluates on the basis of how damaging certain attacks are, how long it takes for those attacks to manifest themselves, and how quickly recovery needs to take place in order to restore service to acceptable levels.

Acknowledgements. This material is based upon work supported by US Army Research Office under contract W911NF-14-C-0140. Any opinions, findings and conclusions or recommendations expressed in this material are those of the authors and do not necessarily reflect the views of the US Army Research Office.

References

1. Jajodia, S., Liu, P., Swarup, V., Wang, C.: Cyber Situational Awareness: Issues and Research. Springer, New York (2010)
2. Kott, A., Wang, C., Erbacher, R.: Cyber Defense and Situational Awareness. Springer, New York (2014)
3. Tyworth, M., Giacobe, N., Mancuso, V., Dancy, C.: The distributed nature of cyber situation awareness. In: IEEE International Multi-Disciplinary Conference on Cognitive Methods in Situation Awareness and Decision Support (2012)

4. Mahoney, S., Roth, E., Steinke, K., Pfautz, J., Wu, C., Farry, M.: A cognitive task analysis for cyber situational awareness. In: Proceedings of the Human Factors and Ergonomics Society Annual Meeting (2010)
5. Pastor, V., Diaz, G., Castro, M.: State-of-the-art simulation systems for information security education, training and awareness. In: IEEE Education Engineering (2010)
6. Rajivan, P.: CyberCog: a synthetic task environment for measuring cyber situation. in Master thesis. Arizona State University (2011)
7. Giacobe, N.A., McNeese, M.D., Mancuso, V.F., Minotra, D.: Capturing human cognition in cyber-security simulations with NETS. In: IEEE International Conference on Intelligence and Security Informatics (2013)
8. Varshney, M., Pickett, K., Bagrodia, R.: A live-virtual-constructive (LVC) framework for cyber operations test, evaluation and training. In: IEEE Military Communications Conference (2011)
9. Cooke, J.N., D'Amic, A., Endsley, R.M., Roth, E., Salas, E.: Perspectives on the role of cognition in cyber security. In: Proceedings of the Human Factors and Ergnomics Society 56th Annual Meeting (2011)
10. D'Amico, A., Whitley, K., Tesone, D., O'Brien, B., Roth, E.: Achieving cyber defense situational awareness: a cognitive task analysis of information assurance analysts. In: Proceedings of the Human Factors and Ergonomics Society Annual Meeting (2005)
11. Panjwani, S., Tan, S., Jarrin, M.K.: An experimental evaluation to determine if port scans are precursors to an attack. In: Proceedings of the 2005 International Conference on Dependable Systems and Networks (2005)
12. Sekar, V., Duffield, N., Spatscheck, O., Merwe, J., Zhang, H.: LADS: large-scale automated DDOS detection system. In: Proceedings of the Annual Conference on USENIX 2006, Annual Technical Conference (2006)
13. Endsley, M.R., Garland, D.J.: Situation Awareness Analysis and Measurement. CRC Press, Boca Raton (2000)

A Cyber Security Multi Agency Collaboration for Rapid Response that Uses AGILE Methods on an Education Infrastructure

Erik Moore[✉] and Dan Likarish

Center for Information Assurance Studies, Regis University,
Denver, CO, USA
{emoore,dlikaris}@regis.edu

Abstract. This study provides a summary and analysis of a cyber security multi agency collaboration for rapid response by Regis University (RU), in partnership with the Colorado Army and Air Force National Guard (CONG) and the State of Colorado (SOC), deploying AGILE methods to improve the ability of the CONG and SOC to respond to attacks against Colorado's critical infrastructure. The summary covers formative discussions and about a year-long series of physical exercises, lectures and certification exams that advanced the study participants domain knowledge, awareness of SOC policy and communication with industry. Other states and territories can use the model to the benefit of their citizens. Events included multiple simulations, physical exercise scenarios, and table top exercises designed to give real-world substance to more abstract cyber security concepts and integrate physical world consequences to actions performed by the participants.

Keywords: Cyber · Security · Multi agency · Collaboration · Rapid response · Agile · Inter-agency · Infrastructure · Physical exercise · Line training · Colorado · Simulation · National guard · State exercise · Constraint · Defense · Operations · Education

1 Introduction

Defense forces operate under highly constrained procedures because of the high impact of their work, their security requirements, and their culture of readiness. This means that training for standard operations is often formulated as standard operating procedure similar to combat *LINE Training* that is highly structured. Cyber conflict, however, operates across multiple types of government and private infrastructure administered with many types of professional practice. As different agencies move to more collaborative and agile defense postures in support of this heterogeneous cyber infrastructure, training exclusively for an independent formal style of operations might overlook significant complexity when preparing to support less structured civilian cyber infrastructure teams who are working in collaborative environments against malicious actors

© IFIP International Federation for Information Processing 2015
M. Bishop et al. (Eds.): WISE9, IFIP AICT 453, pp. 41–50, 2015.
DOI: 10.1007/978-3-319-18500-2_4

whose impetus may turn out to have arisen from organized crime, nation state activity, or loose collaborations of hacktivists. This multiparty scenario creates a highly complex environment where agile collaboration and mutual awareness of differing operational practices would likely be required to achieve high levels of joint capability while maintaining legal boundaries. In the context of this emerging challenge, Regis University invited the leadership of the Colorado National Guard to the Rocky Mountain Collegiate Cyber Defense Competition (RMCCDC) and perceived the value of a more open collaborative training model the RMCCDC and other Regis-hosted competitive and collaborative hands-on events. The Collegiate Cyber Defense Competition (CCDC), developed and organized by the University of San Antonio [1], is a nation-wide cyber defense competition at the college level that has steadily grown to encompass all 50 States in the Union. The approximately seven teams from different institutions are composed of eight to ten students who maintain secure digital services while defending against active cyber attacks and addressing business challenges. In 2012 Regis University joined the CCDC as the last organizational unit, the Rocky Mountain CCDC (RMCCDC) [2]. In consequence of its RMCCDC experience Regis extended the lessons learned from the RMCCDC to its lab-based online and classroom courses, professional user groups and local schools. The CONG leadership, in January 2013, observed a big training advantage in that the types of physical exercises (active scenarios using technology with challenges), tabletop events, and formal lecture training models employed at Regis were not exclusive to any sector or agency. Regis initiated the first effort to leverage this multilaterally compatible structure across agencies and civilian sectors through a successful Information Assurance Scholarship Program Capacity Building grant application submitted to the National Security Agency Education Directorate. The grant application mapped out an extensible model of collaborative capability building activities that would be applicable to the 50 United States of America and related territories. In addition, a significant number of individuals present from other national guard units and law enforcement agencies also participated.

As Steven Cooper *et al.* well expressed the historical context of such efforts, [3] cybersecurity training and education evolved through a wealth of sector-specific training that has matured over the last 40 years, including the CISO-style training that matured into SANS; the information security education programs that perhaps started as early as Queensland Institute of Technology in Australia offered a Master's level research degree in computer security 1986. Cyber security forces capabilities in departments of defense around the world began to mature as evidenced by the expansion of the U.S. Air Force Mission to include cyberspace in 2005. Reference [4] Alternately, a review of trends in cyber investigation as developed by federal and law enforcement [5] provide strong operational capabilities requirements that support the types of skills that would lead to situational awareness in support of effective response to cyber security incidents.

Regis and the other parties initiating this effort set as the primary goal to offer multiple agencies and civilian entities the opportunity to maintain relationships that enable rapid collaborative response and integrated skill development, raising the level of joint capabilities. In context, the collaborative's work extended an earlier ACM education model that places high value on a student's "working knowledge in actually using their skills to interact with the society at large." [6] Individually each participating entity in the collaboration identified their own targeted results. The Colorado National Guard (CONG) expected to leverage the differential between commercial education and internal training to provide a broader experience. The CONG leadership also wanted to achieve a stronger socialization with state and civilian participants. The State of Colorado was expecting to extend their existing training programs and have regular skill-refresh events. Regis was hoping to improve their competition engines, and refine their AGILE-based management structure given a new and broader set of collaborative customers. In addition, Regis expected significant individual knowledge and technical capability benefits of faculty and students who participated in the event.

Regis University provided the technology that facilitated simulation, training, and tool walk-through activities. These include enterprise layer 3 switches, multi-terabyte class production storage network, blade server sets, virtual machine infrastructure, and remote console capabilities provided in team rooms. Regis provisioned this network previously for large multi-team competitive events, research sandbox environments, coursework laboratory space, and industry training events. As Regis deployed diverse configurations in support of this set of applications, the team developed an AGILE-based development and management model.

2   Study Methodology

This study uses case study methodology [7] generally to present and analyze the collaborative efforts from its inception and initial deployment through the current expectations one year after the first event. This study provides background information on the expected needs and describes how the partners managed operation change, developed solutions, and provide mutual review of the outcomes. This study does not provide specific data on the technical outcomes of individual performance, operational details specific to participants, or descriptions of specific technologies used in the specific simulation scenarios as based on interviews, observation, and related references. Also it presents preliminary criteria by which events like this can use for assessment, based on stakeholder objectives.

3   Joint Training Event Design Activities

The leaders of each participating entity contributed specific resources to the effort and exposed specific needs in January of 2013 in order to allow for a collaborative design process based on gap analysis. The Colorado National Guard brought a strong functional cyber security vision and technical security expertise while needing a customized education and a collaborative way to socialize with operations partners in both private and public sectors. The State of Colorado brought a different but overlapping cyber security expertize in addition to their functional requirements. Regis University brought an infrastructure of handling joint physical exercises, a conference facility, and a pool of staff and students to facilitate activities. Regis hoped to use this set of events as an opportunity to improve training facilities and methods, gain faculty and student experience, and further develop the AGILE methodologies that it had begun to use in support of academic computer laboratory infrastructure.

The Xmodel represented in Fig. 1 indicates both the joint effort of the three initial participants and the gateway they represent to larger groups. While the State of Colorado is an exclusive entity, it could also provide this model to other states in support of their own collaborative activities.

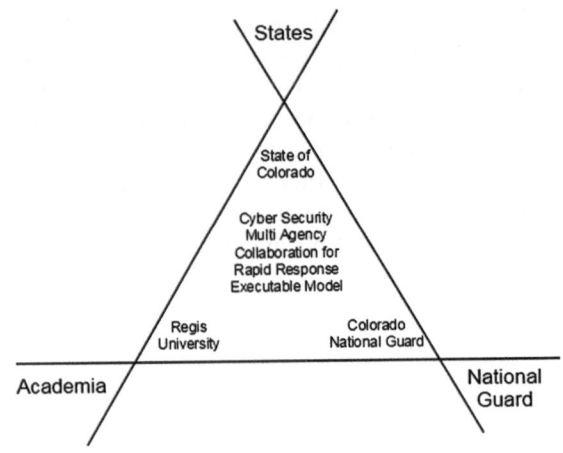

Fig. 1. Initial Xmodel for collaboration and cooperation

The collaborative used many scenarios to build the events, but the primary scenario portrayed the exhaustion of a single private sector or agency's resources and the need to have rapid and well-prepped teams to provide escalated capabilities for incident response. The "Call in the Guard" scenario breaks down into the following steps:

(1) A private entity or group of entities becomes overwhelmed by a cyber security event that has scale and scope significant to the State of Colorado. The entity(s) resources are exhausted and further action is called for.
(2) The private entity calls the State of Colorado to provide assistance.
(3) The Governor's Office assesses the situation and escalates by calling in the Colorado National Guard to provide cyber security support as "cyber smoke jumpers."

In order for this sequence to be successful, well-interfaced lines of communications need to be pre-established and well-tested processes, plans, and roles should be invoked in a collaborative way. During the first collaborative session the leadership team realized that having more active participation from the private sector early on provided greater validation for the simulation and tabletop scenario events. Figure 2 represents the new model for interaction.

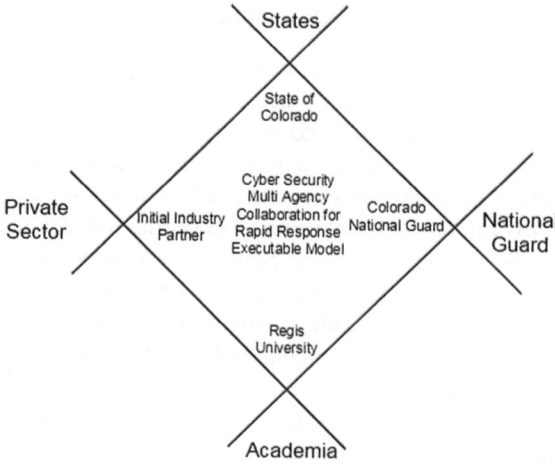

Fig. 2. Updated Xmodel for collaboration and cooperation - includes private sector

To ensure the value of the event for all participants, the formative group performed gap analysis of the sum of the contributed resources in relation to what would be necessary to fulfill the expected needs of each group. The Gap analysis of resources versus needs that took place before the first collaborative event was expected to be speculative at best, and the formative team decided to employ an iterative Agile methodology that provided on-the-fly tuning during events and significant tuning of activities and resources between events.

3.1 Capability Gap Analysis

The joint leadership team focused on the gap between current joint capabilities and desired future capabilities in regards to rapid and agile joint operations as deployed with ad hoc civilian teams that currently protect critical infrastructure. This required that a coordinated response happen rapidly with existing civilian infrastructure teams, and that these teams all be familiar with each other. In support of this the joint leadership team identified within their agencies a need for mutual tool awareness. Considering a higher layer of coordinated incident management, they also set as a goal the coordinated implementation of disparate policies, such that each organization understands the boundaries and professional practices of their partners.

These expected operational needs led to the development of the multi-agency collaboration. The leadership identified through gap analysis the need for a low-pressure training environment that allowed for those policy sets to be meshed in a series of response scenarios. Each group would be aware of how their agency should respond, but would develop an understanding of other agencies' practices and procedures.

3.2   Logistical Hurdles of Inter-Agency Collaboration

As the event came closer, the collaboration leadership team discovered logistical hurdles that were artifacts of the multi-sector effort. The national guard schedule required the events be set on the weekend, while state employees needed to get credit for their time off. The technical team at Regis needed to de-provision some of the technical infrastructure from regular education labs and deploy it exclusively for the weekend virtually overnight. This multi-party coordination challenge existed partly because both the National Guard and the State of Colorado staff saw great value in having the event take place live, face to face, in a location with a minimum of distraction. The physical exercise was the hardest thing to accommodate. The facilities needed a lecture hall large enough for all participants and relatively secure rooms for the teams defending active web services.

Regis University uses a pool of volunteer faculty, students, and partners to facilitate these types of events. Therefore, the Regis Staff works hard not to overburden any individual volunteer. To respond to this issue the Regis team uses an AGILE-based method to build into each development and deployment cycle the specific load of requirements that they are able to handle in one cycle.

3.3   Collaborative AGILE Development Methodology

Over the past 10 years, Regis has been developing an agile process by which infrastructure is maintained and deployed using a very small staff, each with other responsibilities, and a pool of volunteers from the affiliate faculty, alumni, students, and members of the professional community. This situation required an AGILE [8] development model that accommodated a significant flux in human resources, mix of donated, loaned, and core university equipment, and managers. The Regis team named it the Framing Forward Model, and presented it to The Colloquium in 2014. Briefly, it is composed of three layers. In the event layer teams adjust, in real-time, active cyber scenarios to navigate towards successful completion. In the middle Workspace Layer, teams work jointly on a particular project develop scenarios to prepare for events. In the lowest Services layer, the department tracks what human and technical resources are available at any one time to manage demand and allocate resources to project work-spaces. Using that model, the Regis staff and volunteers have met needs for a broad range of events like the Rocky Mountain Collegiate Cyber Defense Challenge, the Information Systems Security and Information systems Auditing and Controls Association professional development events, classroom-supporting laboratory environments, etc. This new challenge of providing cross-sector hands-on events required a new level of agility.

4   Timeline of Events Across First Year of Collaboration

The collaboration included several types of events along the following general timeline. Between these major events the planning team designated intermediate activities where individuals or groups could prepare for upcoming events and focus on skill development in order to enhance their technical contribution to the events. The following bulleted list provides a general timeline of events. The multi-month cycle of learning that this pace incited yielded obvious results in discussions as participants convened at the beginning of each event.

- August 2013 - Event 1 - This event focused on incident response in a red/blue team format. The big lesson learned from this event was that the exercise needed to include more contextual details of operation and success criteria in addition to a standardized technical configuration
- Intermediate time 1 - During this time participants worked on security training, with some completing CISSP and Security + certifications.
- February 2014 - Event 2 - This event focused on cyber forensics and a review of the tools of investigation. Physical exercises included forensic challenges and vendors presented relevant products.
- Intermediate time 2 - During this time participants continued on certifications including Ethical Hacker training.
- August 2014 - Event 3 - This event contained an array of policy, socialization activities, tabletop scenarios, a physical exercise, and malware response review. By this time, participation had grown to include six state guard units, representatives from two Centers of Academic Excellence, and State of Colorado IT and public safety personnel.
- Intermediate time 3 - Participants continue external training and certification in preparation for the next collaborative event.

While the annual timeline is fairly well structured, it is not ridged in that the Regis team adapted the events in real time and debriefed after every event, in order to feed input in to the AGILE development cycle. As new needs became evident, the joint leadership used the intervening time to tune the upcoming collaborative sessions.

5 Joint Exercise - Collaborative Session Components

The Collaborative Leadership Team formulates each session agenda from separate components listed below. The collaboration leaders compiled this component list from pre-existing academic education activities, military exercises, and traditional training methods that each partner brought to the table. However, the content of each component varies from session to session.

- **Partner Mutual Introductions:** This fostered mutual awareness of command hierarchy, jurisdictional boundaries, key standard practices, working vocabulary, and potential hand-off opportunities
- **Physical Exercise:** Participants from each collaborative area looked for hands-on skill improvement in key areas such as protocol analysis, infrastructure awareness and analysis, technology and configuration control, and live incident response. Cross-training of skills and supported introduction of technologies both played significant roles in challenge events.
- **Tabletop Scenario Walk-through:** Key personnel from each sector led a live walk through of a wide variety of scenarios that involved inter-agency hand-off, joint

activities, authority boundary maintenance, and resolution of hierarchy of authority. In addition discussions of escalation options, procedures for accessing resources, and review of role interactions took place as prompted by questions from the participants in the audience. The walk-through led to a significant set of questions regarding governmental response to private sector events and how privacy, intellectual property protection, and access assistance/controls would be handled during events.

- **Technology Reviews:** Private and governmental partners both brought tools to the collaboration by presenting them in review sessions. The tools covered a broad range of areas including the commonly used tools in the commercial world where joint activities are likely to occur. This set ranges from protocol analyzers and event log aggregators to scanners and detection systems.
- **Simulation Challenges:** The Colorado National Guard provided access to a scenario-based participant-vs-machine game that provided challenge events and learning opportunities.
- **Hands-on Formal Tool Training:** Various groups provided specialized forensic, investigation, and defense tools that supported joint operational awareness.

The collaborative leadership maintains and supplements this list in preparation for each major event as needed. Various participants then formulate contents between events. Regis faculty advocated for maximizing re-use and efficiency by structuring modularity at each scale of deployment. This modularity facilitated constructing the event, designing each event component, and tuning the component performance on the fly based on immediate feedback or facilitator awareness of participant issues.

6   Analysis of Outcomes

Generally, the National Guard provided a clear after-action report for the collaborative events. Results of this report proved useful in triggering event improvements as quickly as the very next event. The first major finding was that National Guard team members were organizing their leadership structures internally on an ad hoc basis rather than having it imposed by collaborative leadership or pre-existing rank. The room observers noted that leadership and organization of National Guard teams participating in exercises was not formed with common expectations and in the future this would need to be addressed. The standard organization hierarchy that exists outside the scenarios does not appear to apply in a small-group incident response team as much as experience in technical response and knowledge on incident response procedures.

Second, the team learned that providing a clear process and procedure for self - evaluation and skill assessment yielded significant value. Initially, without clear direction participation in assessments was erratic. The data from those evaluations were used internally by each collaborative entity for identifying training needs of the groups and as a basis for improving the event modules. While the collaborative leadership team did not track participant technical progress individually, they considered that moving to a personalized tracking model might be good. At this time the collaborative leadership team is reviewing logistical and inter-agency policy issues that might present challenges in this area. The specific point in the agenda when post-tests were administered turned out to be significant. The collaborative leadership discovered in the first collaborative event that testing too close to the event end resulted in less participation and loss of attentiveness to detail.

The AGILE method employed by Regis to achieve successful events was not deployed inside the participants' teams during physical exercises. There was a significant delay in some groups particularly when physical exercises began. After discussion with the teams, the gap here may have been because the Regis facilitators were accustomed to working with greater ambiguity of objectives and rapidly self-forming into working groups, so some details had not been sufficiently addressed or described as the scenario was delivered. This suggests that in the future, the team building scenarios will need to design clearer expectations and more detailed structure to more fairly simulate an operational situation.

Developing common vocabulary regarding tools, policy, and logistics turned out to be a big factor linked to the expression of situational needs. Without clear understanding of the full vocabulary involved in a multi-agency situation, miscommunication occurred through assumption or alternative interpretation. With a common vocabulary, efficiency appeared to increase among those groups.

The Colorado Guard had specific desires to cover specific technologies like real-time packet capture analysis, socialize the different groups, ensure all parties understand each sector's leadership hierarchy and roles, and build response team skills and relationships. This went a long way in making the gap analysis effective prior to the collaborative events. Regis' initial requirements were more ambiguous in terms of general improvement of processes, capability, and team knowledge. The challenge for the Regis facilitators was ensuring that the events ran smoothly on a technical and logistical level. The State of Colorado also came with more general goals of collaboration and training, but their early representation in the formative meetings meant that both individual agency and multi-agency collaboration goals would be possible.

7   Conclusion

The Guard, the State of Colorado, and Regis have reaffirmed a strong commitment to continue with the Cyber Security Multi-agency Collaboration for Rapid Response exercises. The collaborative extended the joint effort to more readily include the private sector. Within less than a month after the initial grant review the collaborative leaders established a public-private round table panel linking the public and private sectors. This round table both disseminated results of the grant activities and collected needs from the private sector in order to reset the next round of event goals. The next planned event extends the working relationship and expands the depth and breath of content areas resulting in an advancement of technical, communication and interpersonal skill and knowledge. The collaborative leaders' analysis of the first year's cycle also resulted in refinement of the Xmodel.

The leadership and the technical teams providing training resources continues to successfully use AGILE approaches as part of ongoing collaborative events. The largest adaptation of the AGILE model during the grant period was not in provisioning technical resources for the project, but in controlling a "protocol bleeding" of operational expectations of AGILE methodologies unchecked into assumptions about scenarios. It became clear that because of the need to focus on policy and protocol integration, many functions that the collaborative addressed could not be fulfilled with either AGILE modeling or the Framing Forward Model.

Bibliography

1. White, G.B., Williams, D.: The collegiate cyber defense competition. In: Proceedings of the 9th Colloquium for Information Systems Security Education (2005)
2. Novak, H., Likarish, D., Moore, E.: Developing cyber competition infrastructure using the SCRUM framework. In: Dodge Jr., Ronald C., Futcher, Lynn (eds.) WISE 6, 7 and 8. IFIP AICT, vol. 406, pp. 20–31. Springer, Heidelberg (2013)
3. Cooper, S., Nickell, C., Piotrowski, V., Oldfield, B., Abdallah, A., Bishop, M., Caelli, B., Dark, M., Hawthorne, E., Hoffman, L., Perez, L., Pfleeger, C., Raines, R., Schou, C., Brynielsson, J.: An exploration of the current state of information assurance education. In: Impagliazzo, J. (ed.) Inroads - SIGCSE Bulletin, vol. 41, no. (4), pp. 109–125 (2009)
4. United States Air Force Fact Sheet.: http://www.afspc.af.mil/library/factsheets/factsheet_print.asp?fsID=3649
5. Verison. 2014.: Data breach investigations Report (2014) found at http://www.verizonenterprise.com/DBIR/2014/
6. Hoffman, L., Rosenberg, T., Dodge, R., Ragsdale, D.: Exploring a national cybersecurity exercise for universities. In: Donner, M. (ed.) Security and Privacy, IEEE, 3(5), 27–33 (2005)
7. Smith, N.C.: The case study: a useful research method for information management. J. Inf. Technol. 5(3), 123–133 (1990), ISSN: 02683962. (Routledge, Ltd.) (1990)
8. Manifesto for Agile Software Development. http://agilemanifesto.org/ (2001)

Software Security Education

Cybersecurity Through Secure Software Development

Audun Jøsang[1]([✉]), Marte Ødegaard[2], and Erlend Oftedal[3]

[1] University of Oslo, Oslo, Norway
josang@ifi.uio.no
[2] BEKK Consulting, Oslo, Norway
marte.odegaard@bekk.no
[3] NSense, Oslo, Norway
erlend@oftedal.no

Abstract. Reports about serious vulnerabilities in critical IT components have triggered increased focus on cybersecurity worldwide. Among the many initiatives to strengthen cybersecurity it is common to see the establishment and strengthening of CERTs and other centers for cybersecurity. On the other hand, strengthening education in IT security and applying methods for secure systems development are methods that receive much less attention. In this paper we explain how the lack of focus on security in IT education programs worldwide is a significant contributor to security vulnerabilities, and we propose an agile method for secure software design that requires team members to have received adequate security education and training.

Keywords: Cybersecurity · Security education · Waterfall model · Agile model · Secure agile · Secure software development

1 Introduction

Digitization of business processes and services entails huge savings and increased efficiency. To be sustainable, this development must not at the same time introduce serious security vulnerabilities, but unfortunately it often does. The exposure surface to criminals and other malicious players increases by several orders of magnitude when business processes migrate completely or partially to online platforms. This global exposure to security threats makes it natural to use the term cybersecurity in the sense of protecting assets (information, systems and business processes) that directly or indirectly are connected to the Internet. Robust cybersecurity at all levels is necessary for maintaining a balanced risk profile in a digital economy.

Achieving a secure ICT infrastructure obviously requires that it is designed, built and operated by people who understand the threats, know the security requirements and have the skills to build and operate secure systems in general.

Security vulnerabilities in software are typically caused by programmers or teams with inadequate skills in secure software development. Unfortunately,

M. Bishop et al. (Eds.): WISE9, IFIP AICT 453, pp. 53–63, 2015.
DOI: 10.1007/978-3-319-18500-2_5

thousands of IT designers and experts around the world are lacking security skills precisely because cybersecurity was not part of the study program they followed at the university. The expanding ICT infrastructure worldwide is being built by IT experts with IT degrees from universities and colleges, but unfortunately many IT experts still have insufficient security understanding and expertise. This is an unacceptable situation.

As an analogy, it would of course be irresponsible and even unthinkable to educate building architects and civilly engineers without giving them adequate knowledge about fire safety, otherwise the buildings in which we work and live would be full of firetraps. Likewise it is irresponsible to offer IT programs at universities without compulsory modules in information security. Unfortunately, still today many IT graduates leave university and go into industry without any competence in information security. Despite their great skills in programming and IT design, without skills in security these IT graduates will necessarily build vulnerable IT solutions.

This paper discusses how cybersecurity can be strengthened, not by investing in more sophisticated attack detection and malware filtering tools, but by ensuring that the very foundation of the ICT infrastructure is designed and built for strong security and robustness. This can only be achieved by ensuring that secure system design becomes a natural element in all development projects, and by encouraging, stimulating and maybe forcing technical colleges and universities to integrate mandatory security modules in the curriculum of their IT education programs.

2   Patterns of Cybersecurity

There are currently available on the market a large number of tools and services for strengthening cybersecurity. Vendors range from large and highly profiled companies to small and relatively unknown companies. Some security products are promoted to stop APTs (Advanced Persistent Threats). Other products are promoted to detect and stop singular zero-day attacks or to filter out malware. Intrusion detection and prevention can be bought as a system or as a service. Security governance frameworks such as COBIT[1], ITIL[2], ISO 27001 [6] and NIST SP-800-53 [8] can be adopted and applied by in-house security management staff or by external consultants to ensure that the organisation is managed according to best practice with regard to security. However, none of these tools, services and frameworks – neither in isolation, nor in combination – are sufficient to avoid serious cyber-vulnerabilities of the kind that e.g. Heartbleed, Shellshock and BadUSB represent.

There seems to be no approach that can provide the level of security assurance that governments and corporate managers aim for. In a recent article it is argued that the cybersecurity product market is different from other markets where a few players typically dominate the market [13]. However, for cybersecurity

---

[1] COBIT: Control Objectives for Information and Related Technology.

[2] ITIL: Information Technology Infrastructure Library.

there is no single vendor – not even a set of major vendors – who dominate the cybersecurity market, and from which general cybersecurity solutions can be bought. This simple analysis indicates that cybersecurity does not lend itself to a packaged solution [13].

It is up to the CISO (Chief Information Security Officer) or a similar executive in organisations to set up and run the cybersecurity program as they see appropriate, but since there is no commonly approved product, service or program that can provide waterproof cybersecurity, this task is particularly challenging. Even when following industry best practice there will be vulnerabilities that attackers can exploit to mount successful attacks. In this situation, when a serious security incident occurs, although there often is little the CISO could have done to prevent the incident, the CISO is the obvious target of blame anyway [12]. In a study by the Ponemon Institute focusing on the role of the security manager within companies, many of the CISOs who took part in the study rated their position as the most difficult in the organization. Most of CISOs questioned said their job was a bad one, or the worst job they had ever had [5].

Vulnerability management is an important branch of security management in organisations. Commonly known vulnerabilities are assigned unique identities under the CVE (Common Vulnerabilities and Exposures) scheme started by MITRE Corporation in 1999, with funding from the National Cyber Security Division of the US Department of Homeland Security. CVE IDs are used in SCAP (Security Content Automation Protocol) which is a protocol used by vulnerability management tools. A complete list of CVE IDs can be found on MITRE's CVE system as well as in the US National Vulnerability Database. Prominent software vendors can become a CNA (CVE Numbering Authority) for their products, and each CVE IDs is actually assigned by a CNA. There are three primary types of CNAs:

- The MITRE Corporation functions as Editor and Primary CNA.
- Various CNAs assign CVE IDs for own products (e.g. Microsoft, Oracle, Red Hat).
- Red Hat also provides CVE numbers for open source projects that are not a CNA.

The original CVE-ID format had just four digits for numbering vulnerabilities per year, such as CVE-2014-0160 which identifies the Heartbleed vulnerability. Only allowing 9,999 vulnerabilities per year was seen as a limitation, so that from 2014 the CVE-ID format can have five, six or more end digits to identify an arbitrarily large number of vulnerabilities each year. Figure 1 shows the number of identified vulnerabilities in the CVE scheme during the last 15 years.

The trend seen on Fig. 1 is that the number of vulnerabilities is increasing. There is also a wide range of different vulnerability types, and efforts have been made to provide classifications, taxonomies and ontologies for security vulnerabilities [11]. One purpose of vulnerability classification is to identify weaknesses in the SDLC (Software Development Lifecycle) in order to avoid vulnerabilities in the first place.

# of CVE IDs

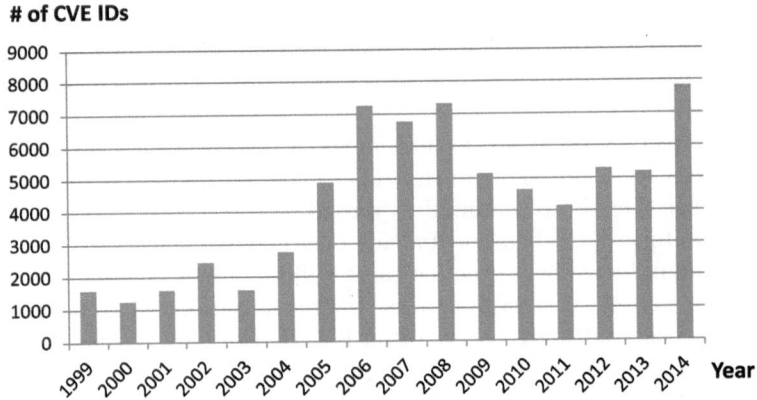

Fig. 1. Number of CVE IDs registered in the period 1999–2014

It is of course impossible to completely avoid generating security vulnerabilities during system and software design. However, the state of cybersecurity can be significantly improved by reducing both the number and the severity of security vulnerabilities generated. The question then is how best to work towards this goal. Several approaches are already used to this end, such as automatic methods that can do code analysis and fuzzing to discover and eliminate vulnerabilities before setting code into production. The most important approach is to follow principles for secure software development, and to ensure that software designers have sufficient security expertise. We discuss the latter approaches below.

3   Software Development Lifecycle

Several software development models or approaches have been proposed and applied during the last 30 years. Each model has its characteristics, advantages and disadvantages, but common to them all is that they are typically not focusing on security [4] (p. 1111). A selection of five prominent development models are briefly analysed and compared in [9]. These are:

- Waterfall model
- Iteration model
- V-shaped model
- Spiral model
- Agile model, aka. XP (Extreme Programming)

The waterfall model is the classical and most heavy-weight approach to software development, whereas the agile model is the most light-weight and flexible approach. We will briefly describe the waterfall and agile models, as they represent very different approaches to secure programming. Figure 2 shows the waterfall model.

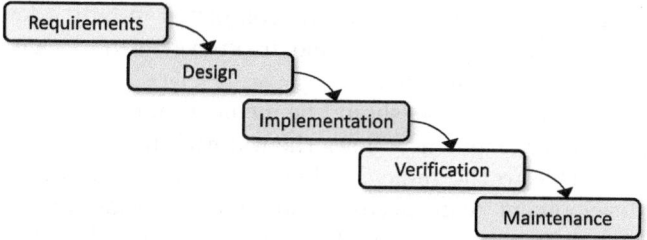

Fig. 2. The waterfall model for software development

The basic idea behind the waterfall model is that the tasks of each phase must be fully completed before the next phase, which is symbolized by the waterfall metaphor where water only flows downwards. This also implies that the complete set of requirements must be defined and fixed at the beginning of the project. In case it is necessary to revisit a previous stage, then a costly overhead is to be expected (metaphorically make water flow upwards), so this should be avoided. However, it is typically the case that requirements have to be changed in the middle of a software development project, so that many software development projects based on the waterfall model have suffered large blow-outs in cost and time.

As a reaction to the rigid structure of the waterfall model several other models have been proposed, where the most recent and radical is the agile model (also known as XP: eXtreme Programming) illustrated in Fig. 3 below.

The basic idea behind the agile model is that new or evolving requirements can be specified in parallel with, or after already implemented requirements [1]. This is possible by splitting the development into separate *stories* where each story covers a set of requirements implemented as functions that can be developed and tested more or less independently of other stories. Each cyclic iteration

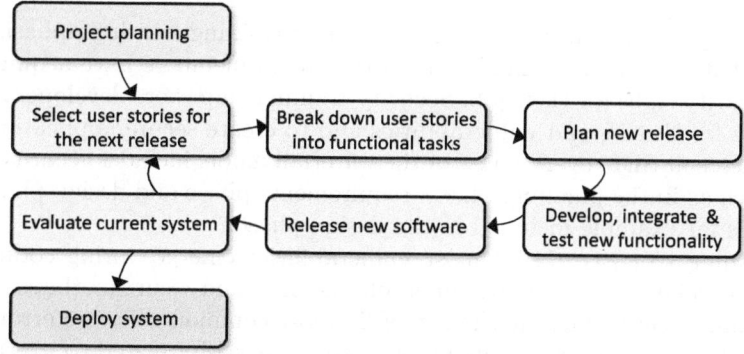

Fig. 3. The agile model for software development

in the agile model is a *sprint* which can be completed in only a few weeks. The major drawback of the agile model is that it often does not scale well to large and complex development projects.

Specific security related tasks should be included in the various phases of the SDLC, whether the development follows the waterfall model, the agile model, or any other model. Due to the radical difference between the waterfall and agile models, the development team needs to adapt the specific approach to secure development depending on the model followed, as described in the next section.

4 Secure Software Development

4.1 Secure Software Development in the Waterfall Model

There are several recommended and 'best practice' models to ensure secure development, including the NIST framework for Security Considerations in the System Development Life Cycle [7], as well as Microsoft's Security Development Lifecycle (SDL) [2] illustrated in Fig. 4 below. Both the NIST model and the Microsoft SDL model are based on the waterfall model for SDLC.

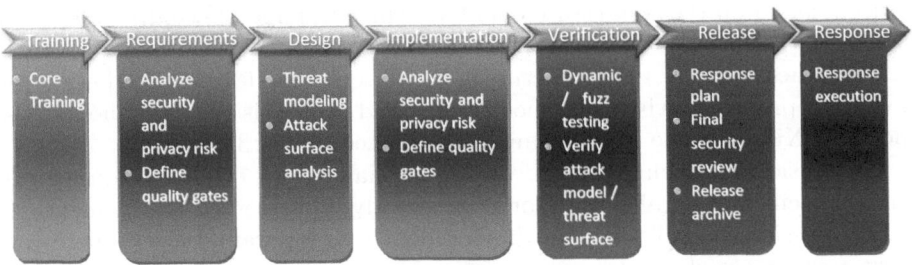

Fig. 4. SDL: Microsoft Security Development Lifecycle [2]

The 1st phase of Microsoft SDL is security training which emphasizes how important it is that programmers and other team members have acquired adequate security skills for their job. Security training empowers developers to have awareness for threats and vulnerabilities and to create secure applications.

In Microsoft SDL, every phase of the waterfall model includes security related tasks, such as in the planning phase, requirements phase and design phase. Risk analysis is for example included in the design phase.

According to [4] (p. 1102) most vulnerabilities emerge during coding. It is therefore crucial that the programmer follows strict and secure methods of secure programming. By looking at the list of 25 most common software errors maintained by SANS[3], we see that many of these are directly related to irresponsible or sloppy programming practice.

---

[3] http://www.sans.org/top25-software-errors/.

4.2   Security Software Development in the Agile Model

There are relatively few studies in the literature on secure agile software development models. In Wichers' proposal [14] it is argued that secure software development in the agile model needs a quite different approach to that of the waterfall model.

In [14] it is recommended to identify all stakeholders and clarify what their main security concerns are. From this analysis a set of threat models can be extracted which in turn form the basis for stakeholder security stories. Then during the development phase, one has periodic security sprints in between the regular development sprints. It is also proposed to include a final security review before deploying the final system.

Microsoft has presented a version of SDL for agile software development [3]. The Agile SDL model contains the same security steps as in the waterfall SDL model, where these steps are grouped in 3 categories:

- One-Time practices: Foundational security practices that must be established once at the start of every new Agile project.
- Every-Sprint practices: Essential security practices to be performed in every sprint.
- Bucket practices: Important security practices that must be completed on a regular basis but can be spread across multiple sprints during the project lifetime.

We find that Microsoft's agiler SDL has merit. However, it has limitations by not separating between functional and non-functional security requirements.

We therefore propose an agile model for secure software development which is partially inspired by the model described in [14] and by Microsoft's Agile SDL model, but which is also an improvement over these because it does not share their disadvantages mentioned above. Our model is also inspired by previous work in [10].

Our approach to handling security in the agile model is based on the distinction between what we call functional security controls and non-functional security controls.

- Functional security controls reflect and implement user stories that are directly related to security, such as when password management and verification is used as a control to implement a user story for logon, or when ACLs (Access Control Lists) are used as a control for specifying and enforcing policies for using various resources within a domain.
- Non-functional security controls are applied in order to eliminate or mitigate vulnerabilities in the implementation of other user stories, such as when applying secure programming techniques in order to avoid buffer overflow bugs, or when applying input filtering when designing a front-end to an SQL database in order to avoid SQL-injection. Software designer must understand that any type of user stories, both ordinary user stories as well as specific security related user stories, must be implemented in a secure way. The way to do that is precisely through non-functional security controls. The idea is that security threats that are intrinsic to a specific user story should be handled during the sprint for the same user story.

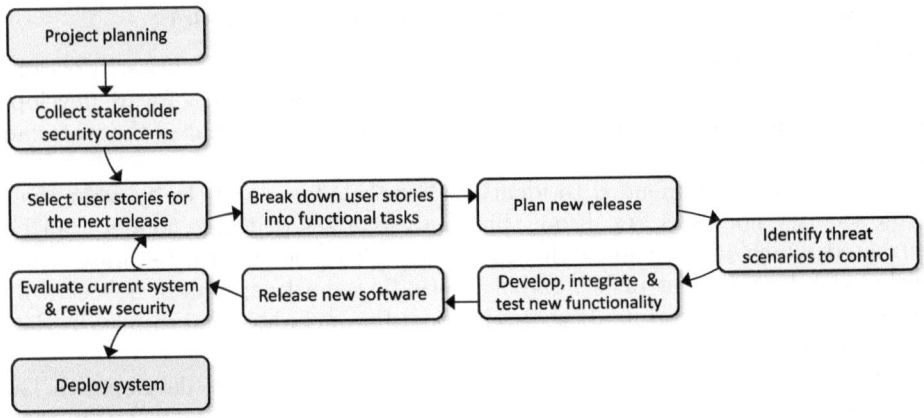

Fig. 5. Proposed model for secure agile software development (Color figure online)

A further example of non-functional security controls is when implementing a user story about the logic for handling the check-out of a shopping basket on an e-commerce website, where a threat could be that the customer is able to trick the system into changing the number of items after the price has been computed, so that he could receive many items but only pay for one. This security concern must be handled during the sprint that implements the check-out of shopping baskets. Based on these considerations we propose to introduce a new security phase into the sprint iteration. This security phase focuses specifically on identifying threats against the current user stories. The new phase should also specify how the threats can be controlled or mitigated, and should specify tests for those mitigation controls. The implementation of non-functional security controls is then handled in the ordinary phase that develops, integrates and tests the new functionality for the current sprint.

Finally, we propose to include a security review in the phase of the sprint iteration cycle where the current version of the system is evaluated. This modified phase, as well as the two new phases that are specific to security, are indicated as yellow boxes in Fig. 5 which illustrates our proposed model for secure agile software development.

It may sometimes be unclear whether a security requirement is functional or non-functional, in which case there is a danger that security requirements are not handled according to the model. The question is what happens when trying to handle functional security as part of other user stories, or when trying to handle non-functional security as a separate user story, which is the opposite of what the model recommends. We analyse these two irregular cases separately below.

– Handling an obvious non-functional security requirement as a functional security requirement would generate unnecessary overhead. This is because non-functional security is an integral part of other user stories, so if non-functional

security is handled separately it would lead to re-iteration of those user stories. Nevertheless, the non-functional security requirements could be adequately taken care of. The conclusion is that development efficiency would suffer, not security.
- In case as an obvious functional security requirements is not handled as a separate user story then the design team has no clear strategy for handling such requirements. At the limit, such functional security requirements could be awkwardly included as a sub-story of other user stories. Alternatively the requirements would not be handled at all, which would be a serious design failure.

If in doubt, it is always safe to consider a security requirement as a separate user story. However, to optimize agility, clearly non-functional security requirements should be integrated as part of other relevant user stories whenever possible.

5 Cybersecurity Training

Security design is challenging, and requires strong skills to get it right. It can therefore not be expected that IT graduates without security training have the necessary skills for developing secure systems. A typical approach to security design in the industry is to let security specialists do a security review of systems that have been developed by software designers without security skills. However, this approach wastes time and manpower. The right approach is to have system designers with security skills who are able to identify vulnerabilities and threat scenarios during the design and development.

It is interesting to notice that in the Microsoft SDL model for secure software design, the 1st phase focuses on security training. In other words, SDL assumed that the design team has acquired security skills before the proper development project starts.

In agile models for secure software design there is no separate phase for security training, neither in the model presented [14] nor in our model presented in Sect. 4.2. For both models it is assumed that team members already have the required knowledge and skills to identify threat scenarios and to craft the corresponding security controls for mitigating those threats. In other words, without security skills among the development team members, no agile model for secure software development would be practical. Given that a large proportion of students following IT programs today still get no or only limited exposure to cybersecurity it is obvious that practicing agile models for secure development is problematic. For this reason there are maturity models for secure software development, where the most prominent are *Building Security In Maturity Model 2* (BSIMM2) and OWASP's *Open Software Assurance Maturity Model* (OpenSAMM).

Governments or interest organisations in many countries are aware of this deficiency and have therefore launched programs to strengthen security education.

In the USA for example, NICE (National Initiative for Cybersecurity Education) established in 2014 builds on the previous Comprehensive National Cybersecurity Initiative started in 2008 as an initiative to strengthen cybersecurity skills in the US federal government sector. NICE has been extended to include the commercial sector, where the goal is to strengthen cybersecurity skills from kindergarten through post-graduate school. The goal of NICE is to establish an operational, sustainable and continually improving cybersecurity education program for the nation to use sound cyber practices that will enhance USA's security.

However, NICE is a US-based imitative and it is still too early to tell how it will influence security education in university IT-programs. The global higher education sector has not yet reached a common consensus that cybersecurity should be an integral part of IT education. In contrast to IT education, in the domain of architecture and civilly engineering education it is obvious that students must acquire knowledge about fire safety. Admittedly there is a difference between these two domains. In architecture and civilly engineering there are strict regulations regarding fire safety, whereas there are no specific regulation for information security in IT systems.

We think initiatives like NICE in the USA should be copied in other countries as well, and could be supported by national computer societies and their umbrella organisation IFIP. National governments could also encourage the higher education sector to strengthen cybersecurity education as part of their IT education programs.

6 Conclusion

There is a consensus in the industry that security must be part of the software development lifecycle. It is not a question of which development model is used, but how well the organisation is able to integrate security in the process.

A weak spot in all the models is that they all depend on the team members having adequate security skills. It can not be expected that every organisation must provide security training to their own staff. Security training must therefore be part of IT education programs in higher education. There is an urgent need to strengthen IT education programs worldwide with regard to cybersecurity. For this purpose it would be interesting to define a security education maturity model for the university sector. If a university offers an IT education program with insufficient security, then that university is part of the problem of causing cybersecurity vulnerabilities. It is time for all IT education institutes to become part of the solution.

References

1. Beck, K. et al.: Manifesto for Agile Software Development, February 2001. www.agilemanifesto.org,
2. Microsoft Corporation. SDL: Microsoft Security Development Lifecycle. Version 4.1 (2009)
3. Microsoft Corporation. Security Development Lifecycle for Agile Development. Version 1.0, 30 June 2009. http://www.microsoft.com/security/sdl/discover/sdlagile.aspx

4. Harris, S.: CISSP All-in-One Exam Guide, 6th edn. McGraw-Hill, New York (2013)
5. Ponemon institute: understaffed and at risk: today's IT security department. Technical report, Ponemon Institute, January 2014
6. ISO. ISO/IEC 27001:2013 - Information technology - Security Techniques - Information security management systems - Requirements. ISO/IEC, 2013
7. Kissel, R. et al.: Security considerations in the system development life cycle - NIST special publication 800-64, Rev. 2. Technical report, National Institute of Standards and Technology, October 2008
8. Joint task force transformation initiative; computer security division; information technology laboratory. security and privacy controls for federal information systems and organizations - NIST special publication 800-53 Rev. 4. Technical report, National Institute of Standards and Technology, April 2013
9. Munassar, N.M.A., Govardhan, A.A.: A comparison between five models of software engineering. Int. J. Comput. Sci. Issues (IJCSI) 7(5), 94–101 (2010)
10. Oftedal, E.: Leveraging agile to gain better security: an agile developer's perspective. In: OWASP AppSec Europe, Poland (2009)
11. Pascal, M.: Handbook of Science and Technology for Homeland Security. Classes of Vulnerabilities and Attacks. Wiley, New York (2007)
12. Perlroth, N.: A Tough Corporate Job Asks One Question: Can You Hack It? New York Times Online 20, July 2014
13. Ross, S.J.: Whiz Bang 2000. ISACA J. 6, 4–5 (2014)
14. Wichers, D.: Breaking the Waterfall Mindset of the Security Industry. In: OWASP AppSec USA, New York (2008)

Security Injections 2.0: Increasing Engagement and Faculty Adoption Using Enhanced Secure Coding Modules for Lower-Level Programming Courses

Sagar Raina[✉], Blair Taylor, and Siddharth Kaza

Department of Computer and Information Sciences,
Towson University, Baltimore, USA
srainal@students.towson.edu,
{btaylor, skaza}@towson.edu

Abstract. Learning interventions based on modules are common in computer science education. Traditional learning modules that present a large amount of content in a linear format can lead to students skimming and skipping content resulting in lower student engagement and effectiveness. In this paper, we present theoretical support for increasing engagement and effectiveness of learning modules, describe a system that implements these principles, and discuss the results of a study across four sections of CS0. Using the Security Injections @Towson cybersecurity modules, we enhanced select modules by incorporating the e-learning design principles of segmentation and interactivity. The study compares student engagement between the current (1.0) modules and the enhanced (2.0) modules. The use of the enhanced (2.0) modules significantly increased student engagement and these results persisted across gender and race. Feedback from instructors indicates higher student and instructor interest in the enhanced modules; in spring 2015, more than 20 instructors are using the enhanced (2.0) modules.

Keywords: Integer overflow · Buffer overflow · Input validation · CS0 · Learning sciences · Interactive learning modules · Instant-feedback · Auto-grading

1 Introduction

The recent focus on cybersecurity education has led to the development of cybersecurity learning materials across various academic institutions and organizations in the United States [19]. Among such initiatives are web-based learning modules developed by the Security Injections @Towson project [5, 13, 17]. These learning modules target key secure coding concepts including integer error, buffer overflow, and input validation in various programming languages, for Computer Science 0 (CS0), Computer Science 1 (CS1), and Computer Science 2 (CS2); and general security concepts, such as phishing, passwords, and cryptography for use in Computer Literacy courses. The Security Injections @Towson modules have been found to be highly effective at improving security awareness and the ability to apply secure coding concepts [13]. In over six years

© IFIP International Federation for Information Processing 2015
M. Bishop et al. (Eds.): WISE9, IFIP AICT 453, pp. 64–74, 2015.
DOI: 10.1007/978-3-319-18500-2_6

of dissemination to over 150 institutions, the following issues have been observed: (1) instructors noted that students tended to skip content and proceed directly to lab exercises, and (2) large-scale adoption by instructors remains a challenge.

The modules originally developed in the project are web-based learning modules that follow a traditional linear format (we refer to these as 1.0 modules hereafter). This type of module design, that presents a large amount of content at one time, is common in many disciplines, but can lead to issues like skimming and skipping [11, 16]. In this paper, we discuss the key issues that lead to skipping and skimming, including the amount of content presented on a screen and decreased student engagement. Presenting less content allows students to process information more easily and improves learning; increasing student engagement motivates students to learn [1, 2, 9, 11, 12, 16, 18]. We describe enhanced modules, Security Injections 2.0, that address these issues by utilizing segmentation and interactivity, and a study that tests the engagement of the new modules. In addition, the enhanced modules include an auto-grading functionality to facilitate easier instructor adoption.

To assess the effectiveness of enhanced learning modules towards student engagement and instructor adoption, we compare the Security Injections 1.0 modules to 2.0 and explore the following questions:

Q1: How can we improve the traditional web-based learning modules to reduce content skipping, increase engagement and instructor adoption?

Q2: Can the use of 2.0 modules with segmentation and interactivity increase student engagement compared to the 1.0 modules?

Q3: Can the use of 2.0 modules with auto-grading increase instructor adoption compared to the 1.0 modules?

2 Literature Review

Web-based learning modules present content using hypertext. Individuals reading hypertext have a tendency to skip or skim the content [14]. In this section, we discuss: (1) why hypertext readers skip or skim the content, and (2) how can we improve interactivity in learning modules to engage learners.

2.1 Hypertext Reading and Content Skipping

Hypertext is text that contains links to text, audio, video, or graphics in other documents or media resources, giving flexibility to readers to click any of the links to gain knowledge [3]. Hypertext readers often adopt a reading strategy which determines what to read and what to skim [3, 7]. This may lead more selective reading for lengthy documents. Readers who skim have a tendency to read the first half of the paragraph and if they determine that the gain of information is low, they may skip the other half of the paragraph and jump to the next paragraph [4]. This skipping may lead readers to lose important information [4, 11]. Selective reading may also lead to less in-depth reading, less concentration and attention towards the content [8]. In addition, skipping of the content leads to poor learning [12].

Research suggests that instead of presenting large amounts of hypertext content at once, the content should be broken into smaller chunks and presented one idea at a time on a single screen [1, 2, 9]. This concept is referred to as segmentation. Segmentation improves processing of information in the working memory and makes recalling and retention of concepts easier [9].

2.2   Improving Interactivity in Learning Modules

Interactivity in e-learning is the "responsiveness to the learner's actions during learning" [9, 18]. Interactivity improves engagement and motivates students to learn [18]. The types of interactivity in e-learning environments include: dialoguing, controlling, manipulating, searching and navigating [9]. In this paper, we focus on dialoguing and controlling.

Increasing Interactivity with Dialoguing - Dialoguing occurs when the learner answers questions and receives feedback to his/her input. Dialoguing has been considered beneficial, as learners can relate the feedback to the current content [15]. In e-learning, dialoguing can be implemented using assessments (like formative questions) with appropriate feedback [15]. This assessment can be conducted using multiple-choice, fill-in-the-blank, short answer and essays formats. The feedback provided on the answers can be either immediate or delayed. The feedback provided can also be classified based on the amount of detail provided on the answers [6, 15] and is categorized as: (1) *Knowledge of Results (KR)*, (2) *Knowledge of Correct Response (KCR)* and, 3) *Elaborate Feedback (EF)*.

Knowledge of results (KR) informs the learner if their answer is correct or incorrect; knowledge of correct response (KCR) informs if the answer is correct or incorrect and includes the correct answer; and elaborate feedback (EF) informs if the answer is correct or incorrect, includes the correct answer, and also includes a concise explanation of the correct answer.

We plan to implement dialoguing in 2.0 modules using Multiple Choice Questions (MCQs), true or false and constructed response (CR) type of assessments with immediate knowledge of results (KR) and immediate elaborate feedback (EF).

Increasing Interactivity with controlling - Controlling implies that the learner can determine the pace of the presentation. Controlling helps students learn better by allowing them to process information at their own pace [2, 9]. We plan to implement controlling in 2.0 modules using answer-until-correct [15] with immediate knowledge

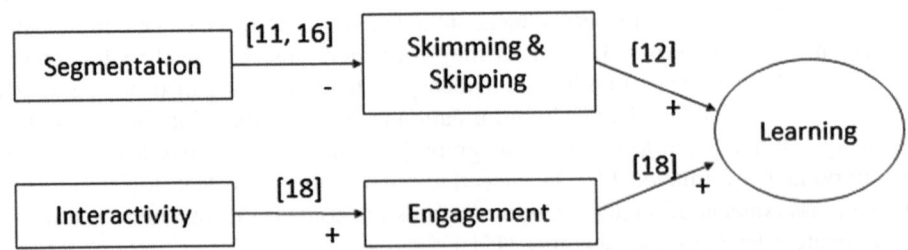

Fig. 1. Literature suggests that segmentation and interactivity in modules may increase learning

of results (KR) and immediate elaborate feedback (EF) to MCQs, true or false and constructed response (CR) type of assessments.

Segmentation breaks large content into smaller chunks and presents them one at a time which may result in less reading and less skipping of content. Less skipping of content leads to increased learning [12]. Interactivity (dialoging and controlling) on segmented chunks leads to engagement and enforces learning (see Fig. 1.).

3 Incorporating Segmentation, Instant-Feedback and Auto-Grading in Security Injection Modules

The Security Injection learning modules 1.0 were developed on the cognitive learning principles of Bloom's taxonomy and adopt a uniform structure. Each module begins with a background section to describe the problem with examples, followed by a "Code Responsibly" section (that includes methods to avoid security issues), a laboratory assignment with a security checklist, and discussion questions. The module structure is designed to help students to first understand the problem through the background and code responsibly sections, remember it through the laboratory assignments, evaluate it through checklists, and apply the concepts learned through discussion questions.

In the 2.0 modules, we enhanced the 1.0 modules by applying segmentation to reduce skipping of content, and interactivity, using dialoging and controlling, to improve student engagement. We implemented segmentation by breaking up the module content per section (background, code responsibly, laboratory assignment, discussion questions) and presenting each section, one at a time, on the screen (see Fig. 2.). We implemented dialoguing using formative assessment including true or false, multiple choice and constructed response that include immediate knowledge of results (KR) or elaborate feedback (EF). We implemented controlling using answer-until-correct giving the students control over the number of attempts. Students receive immediate knowledge of results (KR) feedback until third attempt and immediate elaborate feedback (EF) thereafter.

Module Design - In the background and code responsibly sections, students are required to go through the content and answer a set of checkpoint questions. Each question provides immediate feedback on submit (see Figs. 3 and 4.). The student cannot advance to the next section until all questions are answered correctly. In the laboratory assignment and discussion question, students answer text-based, multiple choice questions, and identify vulnerabilities based on a security checklist (see Fig. 5.). These are also auto-graded.

System Implementation - To implement the enhanced modules, several solutions were considered (including writing the system from scratch) before determining that a modified version of Stanford University's class2go web-based application (https://github.com/Stanford-Online/class2go/) was most appropriate. Class2go is built using the Django framework. Class2go is an open-source framework that provides core functionality, including user registration, course creation, test administration, and some components for auto-grading. We wrote code to auto-grade the security checklist, and regular expressions that match keywords to verify answers for short-answer questions (constructed response). In addition, we developed an instructor dashboard with a progress grade-book to monitor student progress (see Fig. 6.).

CS0 - C++ - Integer Error

Integer Error –"You Can't Count That High" - CS0

Background
Summary:

Integer values that are too large or too small may fall outside the allowable range for their data type, leading to undefined behavior that can both reduce the robustness of yc

Fig. 2. Modules broken into sections

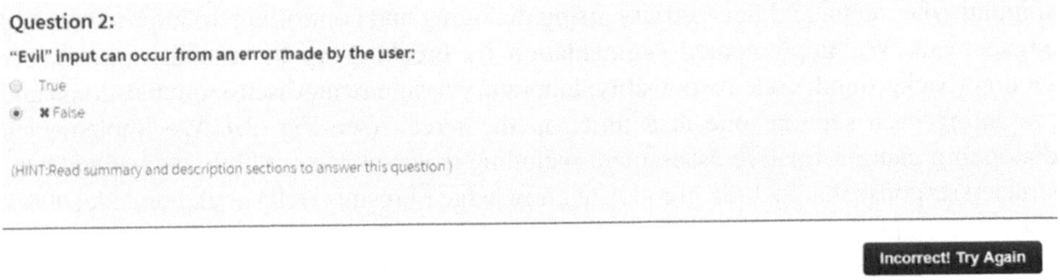

Question 2:

"Evil" input can occur from an error made by the user:

○   True

●   ✘ False

(HINT:Read summary and description sections to answer this question)

Incorrect! Try Again

Fig. 3. Instant-feedback on incorrect answer

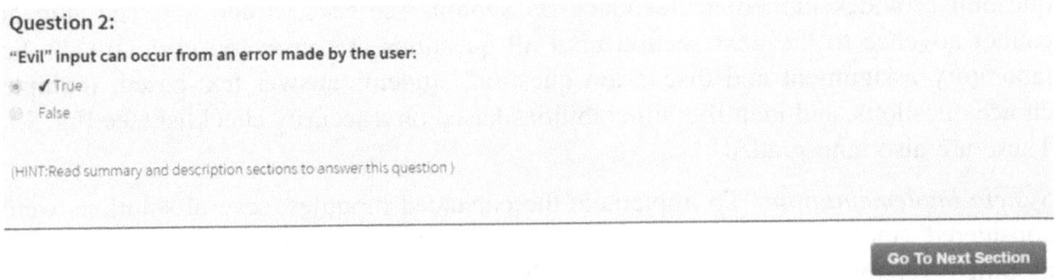

Question 2:

"Evil" Input can occur from an error made by the user:

●   ✓ True

○   False

(HINT:Read summary and description sections to answer this question)

Go To Next Section

Fig. 4. Instant-feedback on correct answer

```
#include <iostream>
#include <limits>
using namespace std;
int main(void)
{

    int i;
    int j;

    cout << "For this compiler: " << endl;
    cout << "integers are: " << sizeof (int) << " bytes " << endl;
    cout << "largest integer is " << INT_MAX << endl;
    cout << "smallest integer is " << INT_MIN << endl;

    cout << "Input two integer values " << endl;
    cin >> i >> j;

    cout << endl << "You entered the following values: " << endl;
    cout << "integer " << i << " " << j << endl;

    int result = i * 10;
    cout << "Your number times ten is " << result << endl;
    result = i + j;
    cout << "The sum of your numbers is " << result << endl;
    result = i * j;
    cout << "The product of your number is " << result << endl;

    return 0;
}
```

Vulnerability: *Integer Errors* **Course:** *CS0*	
Check each line of code	Completed
1. Click each declaration of an integer variable.	✓
For each variable from 1:	
2. Click all input operations that assign values to the variable.	✓
3. Click all mathematical operations involving the variable.	✓
4. Click all assignments made to the variable.	✓
Highlighted areas indicate vulnerabilities!	

Fig. 5. Auto-graded security checklist

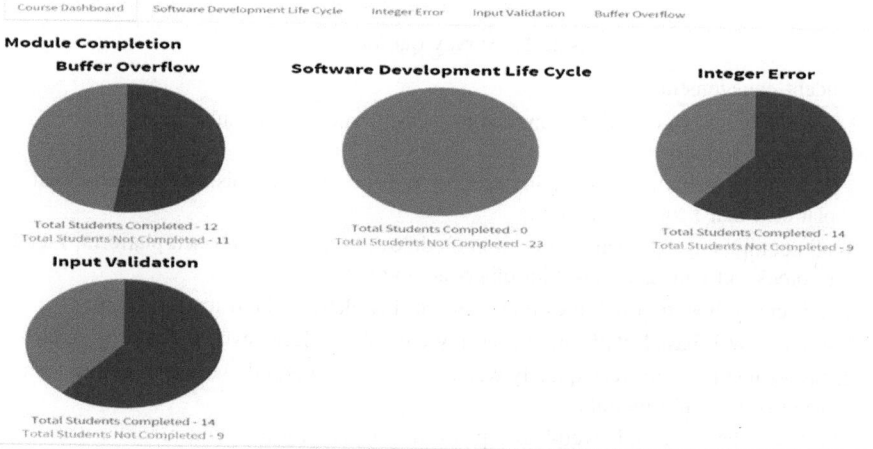

Fig. 6. Instructor grade-book

4 Study

4.1 Methodology

A quasi-experimental study was conducted in fall 2014 across four sections of a CS0 course (using C++) at a large public university, using a posttest only control group design. Two of the sections used the 1.0 version (control group) and the other used 2.0 (treatment group). The study was conducted during the laboratory sessions which were at different times for each section. Three modules - integer error, input validation and buffer overflow - were introduced, in that order, with approximately four weeks between the interventions. Both groups were administered a student engagement survey at the end of the semester.

The survey instrument used in this study measured student demographics and student engagement. While questions related to student demographics were derived from previous security injection studies [13], which measured students' gender, age-group, ethnicity and major, we adapted a set of eight item questions from a well-tested User Engagement Scale (UES) [10] to measure student engagement. The eight item student engagement questions were recorded on a five point Likert scale. (See Table 1 for sample survey questions.)

Based on the survey scores, we proposed the following hypothesis to compare Security Injections 1.0 and Security Injections 2.0 (treatment group) on the following dependent variable: student engagement score.

H1: The mean of survey scores for student engagement in the treatment group will be significantly higher than the mean of the survey scores for student engagement in the control group.

Table 1. Survey questions

	Student engagement
Q1	I felt deeply engrossed while completing security injection modules using this web-based platform
Q2	I get so involved while completing security injection modules using this web-based platform that I forget everything
Q3	While completing the security injection modules using this web-based platform, I tend to block out conversations with others around me
Q4	The Security Injection modules presented on this platform hold my attention
Q5	Using this web-based platform excited my curiosity to learn cybersecurity principles
Q6	Time seemed to go by very quickly when I use this web-based platform for completing Security Injection module
Q7	The screen layout of this web-based platform for Security Injection modules was visually pleasing
Q8	Using this web-based platform for completing Security Injection modules was attractive

4.2 Initial Results

A total of 116 students participated in the study. After filtering missing data and outliers, 80 (42 in the treatment group and 38 in the control group) students including 54 (29 in the treatment group and 25 in the control group) males and 26 (13 in the treatment group and 13 in the control group) females completed the survey. For student engagement, each response was assigned codes from 1 to 5, on a five point Likert scale, 1 representing 'strongly disagree' and 5 representing 'strongly agree'. The engagement score for each respondent were calculated as the mean of codes for eight questions. The Cronbach's alpha, for eight-item engagement questions, was found to be 0.74, which suggested good internal consistency. The hypothesis was tested using independent samples t-test. We picked independent samples t-test because Shapiro-Wilk test showed that scores for student engagement in both the groups (treatment n = 42, control n = 38) satisfied the conditions of normal distribution (treatment p = .593, control p = .187) and homogeneity of variance (F = 2.554, p = .114 > 0.05).

Comparison of survey scores for student engagement in treatment and control groups.
In the survey results, the mean score for the treatment group (n = 42, mean = 3.43) was found to be significantly higher at 95 % level (t = −2.265, p = 0.026) than the mean score for the control group (n = 38, mean = 3.19). This implies that students found Security Injections 2.0 more engaging than Security Injections 1.0 (see Fig. 6a.). This leads us to accept H1 and supports research question Q2. In addition, higher engagement persisted across gender (see Fig. 6b.) and race (see Fig. 6c.).

Comparing results for individual survey questions between control and treatment groups.
The student engagement mean score for the treatment group was found to be higher than the control group (see Table 2). In particular, the scores for Q6 and Q8 were found to be statistically significant at 95 % level (refer to Table 1 for survey questions).

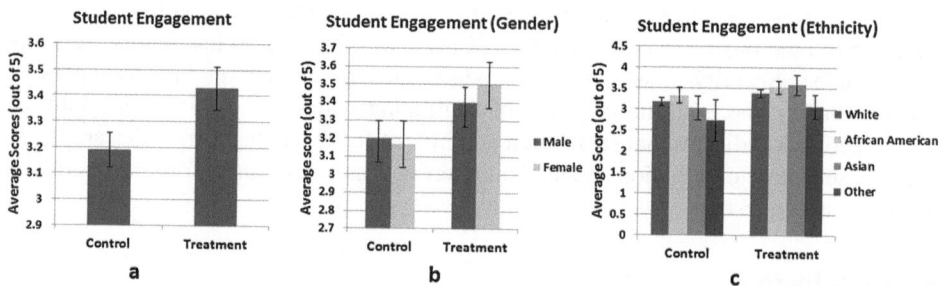

Fig. 6. (a) Average student engagement score in treatment and control group (b) Average student engagement score between males and females in treatment and control group (c) Average student engagement score between ethnic groups in treatment and control group

Table 2. Results of individual survey questions

	Mean score	
	Control (n = 38)	Treatment (n = 42)
Q1	3.39	3.48
Q2	2.63	2.74
Q3	2.89	3.07
Q4	3.37	3.45
Q5	3.34	3.33
Q6	3.08	3.79*
Q7	3.50	3.79
Q8	3.29	3.79*
Student Engagement Mean Score	**3.19**	**3.43***

*$p < 0.05$ (statistically significant at 95 % level)

5 Instructor Feedback

Security Injections 2.0 modules were introduced to over 50 faculty members in workshops conducted last year. In the past year, five instructors have used the beta system for both in-class and online instruction to approximately 180 students. Introduction of the modules at the workshops has led to overwhelmingly positive response among instructors who look forward to incorporating the 2.0 modules in their curriculum, primarily due to the auto-grading functionality. One workshop attendee indicated, "I am excited about the interactive modules (injection 2.0). I will be more likely to incorporate these modules." An instructor who used both versions of Security Injections modules in a class of 30 students in summer 2014 commented, "The students were able to access the materials easily, and seemed to enjoy the interactive modules more. They were also able to get feedback faster, and seemed more comfortable with it compared to the other version." In spring 2015, approximately 20 instructors are using 2.0 modules. Security Injections 2.0 modules are developed on the principles of learning theory and with the intention of facilitating wide-spread instructor adoption. Initial feedback indicates that segmented and instant-feedback based modules are likely to increase instructor adoption and student interest, which supports our initial result and third research question.

6 Conclusion

In this study, we designed a system of enhanced secure coding learning modules that implement the principles of segmentation; by breaking content from 1.0 into individual sections per screen with checkpoint questions, and interactivity; by including instant-feedback. We conducted a study to test their effectiveness towards increasing student engagement across four sections of CS0 using the post only control group design. In addition, we collected instructor feedback.

Results from the study showed the segmented and interactive 2.0 modules led to significant increase in student engagement. Additionally, higher engagement persisted across gender and race. Feedback from instructors indicates both higher student and instructor interest. In addition, the increase in use of enhanced modules by instructors indicated higher instructor adoption.

Due to the limited instruments available to assess whether segmentation leads to less skipping and skimming, we plan an observational study in fall 2015 to record student behavior using segmented and interactive modules.

In addition, in future work, we plan a full scale experiment across multiple sections and courses, to examine the effectiveness of the enhanced modules, towards our goal of increasing secure coding knowledge among computer science students.

Acknowledgements. Class2go (https://github.com/Stanford-Online/class2go/). This project is partially supported by NSF DUE-1241738.

References

1. Al-Samarraie, H., et al.: Can structured representation enhance students' thinking skills for better understanding of E-learning content? Comput. Educ. **69**, 463–473 (2013)
2. Clark, R.C., Mayer, R.E.: e-Learning and the Science of Instruction: Proven Guidelines for Consumers and Designers of Multimedia Learning (Google eBook). Wiley, San Francisco (2011)
3. DeStefano, D., LeFevre, J.-A.: Cognitive load in hypertext reading: A review. Comput. Human Behav. **23**(3), 1616–1641 (2007)
4. Duggan, G.B., Payne, S.J.: Skim Reading by Satisficing: Evidence from Eye Tracking. In: Proceedings of the International Conference on Human Factors in Computing Systems, CHI 2011, Vancouver, BC, Cananda (2011)
5. Kaza, S., et al.: Injecting Security in the Curriculum: Experiences in Effective Dissemination and Assessment Design. The Colloquium for Information Systems Security, Education (CISSE) (2010)
6. Van der Kleij, F.M., et al.: Effects of feedback in a computer-based assessment for learning. Comput. Educ. **58**(1), 263–272 (2012)
7. Lawless, K.A., et al.: Knowledge, Interest, Recall and Navigation: A Look at Hypertext Processing. J. Lit. Res. **35**, 911–934 (2003)
8. Liu, Z.: Reading behavior in the digital environment: Changes in reading behavior over the past ten years. J. Doc. **61**(6), 700–712 (2005)
9. Moreno, R., Mayer, R.: Interactive multimodal learning environments. Educ. Psychol. Rev. **19**(3), 309–326 (2007)
10. O'Brien, H.L., Toms, E.G.: The development and evaluation of a survey to measure user engagement. J. Am. Soc. Inf. Sci. Technol. **61**(1), 50–69 (2010)
11. Protopsaltis, A., Bouk, V.: Towards a Hypertext Reading/Comprehension Model. In: SIGDOC'05 (2005)
12. Rudestam, K.E., Schoenholtz-Read, J. eds: Handbook of Online Learning. SAGE Publications (2010)
13. Taylor, B., Kaza, S.: Security injections: modules to help students remember, understand, and apply secure coding techniques. In: Proceedings of the 16th annual joint conference on Innovation and technology in computer science education - ITiCSE 2011, p. 3. ACM Press, New York, USA (2011)

14. Taylor, J.S.: Using the World Wide Web in Undergraduate Geographic Education: Potentials and Pitfalls. J. Geog. **99**(1), 11–22 (2000)
15. Thalheimer, W.: Providing Learners with Feedback—Part 1: Research-based recommendations for training, education, and e-learning. Somerville, Massachusetts (2008)
16. Tseng, M.: The Difficulties That EFL Learners Have with Reading Text on the Web. Internet TESLJ. **14**, 2 (2008)
17. Turner, C.F. et al.: Security in Computer Literacy- A Model for Design, Dissemination, and Assessment. In: Proceedings of the 42nd ACM technical symposium on Computer science education - SIGCSE 2011, p. 15. ACM Press, New York, USA (2011)
18. Zhang, D.: Interactive Multimedia-Based E-Learning: A Study of Effectiveness. (2010)
19. Curriculum Resources - Teaching Tools for Educators, http://niccs.us-cert.gov/education/curriculum-resources

The Use of Software Design Patterns to Teach Secure Software Design: An Integrated Approach

Johan van Niekerk[✉] and Lynn Futcher

Nelson Mandela Metropolitan University, Port Elizabeth, South Africa
{Johan.VanNiekerk,Lynn.Futcher}@nmmu.ac.za

Abstract. During software development, security is often dealt with as an add-on. This means that security considerations are not necessarily seen as an integral part of the overall solution and might even be left out of a design. For many security problems, the approach towards secure development has recurring elements. Software design patterns are often used to address a commonly occurring problem through a "generic" approach towards this problem. The design pattern provides a conceptual model of a best-practices solution, which in turn is used by developers to create a concrete implementation for their specific problem. Most software design patterns do not include security best-practices as part of the generic solution towards the commonly occurring problem. This paper proposes an extension to the widely used MVC pattern that includes current security principles in order to teach secure software design in an integrated fashion.

Keywords: Information security education · Secure software design · Secure software development · Software design patterns

1 Introduction

During software development, security is often dealt with as an add-on. This means that security considerations are not necessarily seen as an integral part of the overall solution and might even be left out of a design. Recently some efforts have been made to "shift some of the focus in security from finding bugs to identifying common design flaws" (http://cybersecurity.ieee.org/center-for-secure-design.html). However, efforts such as the IEEE centre for secure design is still relatively new and much work in this regard remains.

For many security problems, the approach towards secure development has recurring elements. Software *design patterns* are often used to address a commonly occurring problem through a "generic" approach towards this problem. The design pattern provides a conceptual model of a best-practices solution, which in turn is used by developers to create a concrete implementation for their specific problem.

The use of such design patterns has several major advantages. Firstly, the pattern provides a guideline towards best-practice. Secondly, the use of the pattern provides developers with a shared vocabulary that enables them to communicate complex design concepts easily and clearly. Due to these, and other benefits, design patterns are often taught in software design courses. Most software design patterns do not include **security**

© IFIP International Federation for Information Processing 2015
M. Bishop et al. (Eds.): WISE9, IFIP AICT 453, pp. 75–83, 2015.
DOI: 10.1007/978-3-319-18500-2_7

principles as part of the generic solution towards the commonly occurring problem. This paper proposes an extension to the widely used MVC pattern that includes current security principles in order to teach secure software design in an integrated fashion.

2   Teaching Secure Software Development

Khan and Mustafa [1] define secure software as: '*software that is able to resist most attacks, tolerate the majority of attacks it cannot resist, and recover quickly with a minimum of damage, from the very few attacks it cannot tolerate*'.

According to Burley and Bishop [2], there is an ever-increasing demand for software systems that are resilient, reliable and secure. They state that '*secure software development is a deep and tremendously important subject. Many problems arise from not focusing on the security aspects of software development*' [2].

Many software security vulnerabilities are not coding issues at all but design issues [3]. In order to meet the demands, opportunities and threats associated with software development, security needs to be integrated into the overall software development life cycle. However, the reality is that security is often perceived as a barrier to functionality, adding constraints and reducing flexibility. Software developers generally ignore the idea of security or consider it as an afterthought. This typically leads to software applications having many security flaws and weaknesses.

Microsoft authors Howard and LeBlanc [4], in support of secure software development, stress that software developers should avoid adding security as an afterthought for the following reasons:

- Adding any feature (including security) as an afterthought, is expensive;
- Adding security later may change the way features have been implemented. This, too, is expensive;
- Adding security later involves wrapping security around existing features, rather than designing features with security in mind; and
- Adding security as an afterthought may change the application interface, which may, in turn, break the code that has been used to rely on the current interface.

Taylor and Azadegan [5] support this notion, and state that: '*building secure systems requires incorporating security principles early and often throughout the software development life cycle*'. Information security should, therefore, be an integral part of the development process; and it should be taken into account at every stage of the software development life cycle.

In addition, software developers need to use improved practices that consistently produce secure software. Such practices should measurably reduce software specification, design and implementation defects; thereby, minimizing any potential risks. The development of secure software requires knowledge and techniques not commonly taught or practiced by most software developers [1].

In a report on the Summit on Education in Secure Software, Burley and Bishop [2] summarise some fundamental factors to ensure secure software development, namely:

- Understanding security, especially during design, requires a holistic approach;
- Programmers and non-programmers must be educated in the core principles and practices of secure software design;
- The principles of secure programming must be integrated into a curriculum designed to meet the cyber security challenges of the future; and
- Secure programming must be considered within the context of the full system design and deployment process.

According to Heyman, Yskout, Scandariato and Joosen [6], in the security discipline, a well-known principle calls for the use of standard, time tested solutions rather than inventing ad hoc solutions from scratch. Various researchers propose that security patterns can potentially contribute significantly to the design and development of secure software, since they provide re-usable solutions to security problems, and incorporate expert knowledge. However, Yoshioka, Washizaki and Maruyama [7] state that: *'although various security patterns and techniques for using them have recently been proposed, it is still difficult to adapt them to each phase of the software development life cycle'*. Further research is therefore required to address the use of patterns within the software development life cycle in order to ensure that security concerns are integrated into the development process.

3   Teaching Advanced OO and Design Patterns

One of the benefits of the Object Orientated Programming (OOP) paradigm is that it allows software developers to reuse source code. Such reuse is supposed to bring many benefits, including increased productivity, improved code quality, and more design consistency [8]. In software development problems often recur, but not necessarily in the same context. Due to this difference in context, code reuse is not always practical since the different contexts of the problems might prevent the reuse of existing code without substantial modification.

In order to reuse a software solution, one would need a general solution that can be adapted to the specific problem's context. Such general solutions are not necessarily always possible in terms of reusable code, however it is often still possible to package domain-independent knowledge and expertise in a reusable way in the form of software design patterns [6].

A pattern can be described as *'a solution to a problem in a context'* [9]:

- The context is the situation in which the pattern applies. This should be a recurring situation;
- The problem refers to the goal you are trying to achieve in this context, but it also refers to any constraints that occur in the context [9];
- The problem should be a recurring problem [10];
- The solution provides a general design (core solution) that extracts the essence of the solution to resolve the problem for the given context and constraints [9, 10].

Software designers rarely start a new design from first principles. Instead they rely on existing designs to inform the new solution. Design patterns provide a commonly used mechanism, or shared vocabulary to communicate such previous solutions to commonly occurring problems. It is important to note that a design pattern is not a finished design that can be transformed directly into code [11]. Instead, it provides a "template" for the solution that can be adapted to the problem's specific context [11]. Design patterns provide software designers with three main advantages:

- Firstly, the solution is known to be sound because it is time-tested;
- Secondly, benefits and drawbacks of a pattern are known in advance and they can be taken into account while sketching the solution;
- Thirdly, patterns establish a common vocabulary that can ease communication between different stakeholders [6, 10].

These advantages also make patterns very useful in the teaching of software design. Many complex system frameworks make extensive use of design patterns to provide basic underlying services within the framework. Knowledge of the underlying design patterns is often assumed, and used to aid in explanations regarding scalability, modularity, extensibility, etc. within these frameworks [11]. Such knowledge will, however, only aid in the discussions of complex frameworks if students *understood the intent and implementations of each of the design patterns separately before combining them* [11].

Design patterns can thus be seen as an important tool in the communication of knowledge regarding good software design. However, due to the need to present design patterns as a general template that is not specific to a particular context, most design patterns do not by default include any aspects related to secure software development. To a certain extent this exacerbates the problem of teaching secure software development since security should ideally not be dealt with as an optional add-on in a software design. Instead, systems should be designed as secure systems from the ground up. It would thus be beneficial for the teaching of secure software design, to have design patterns that incorporate basic secure design principles as an integral part of the pattern itself. Many design patterns could probably be adapted to include security concerns, however, this paper will only focus on one such pattern, the Model-View-Controller (MVC) pattern. The MVC pattern is widely used in modern software development and is especially useful in designs for a distributed n-tier architecture, which makes it an ideal pattern for the design of many online applications. As such this pattern was deemed appropriate for use in this paper.

4 Integrating Secure Design Principles into the Model-View-Controller (MVC) Pattern

The MVC pattern forms the basis for the very popular n-tier approach towards software design and is thus often taught in software design courses. The pattern is a compound pattern which uses other patterns to provide specific "services" to the design. The MVC separates the design and development of the user interface (View) from the underlying controlling logic for this view (Controller), which is further separated from the problem domain's underlying state, data, and application logic (Model) [9]. The structure of the MVC pattern works to separate the responsibilities of components and is especially well suited to web applications [12].

The View shows the windows, buttons, and other controls to the user; the Controller interprets clicks and other commands; and the Model does the business logic and object retrieval – then relaying the changes to the View again [12]. The View can request state information from the Model, and the Controller can ask the View to update its display. This relationship is shown in Fig. 1.

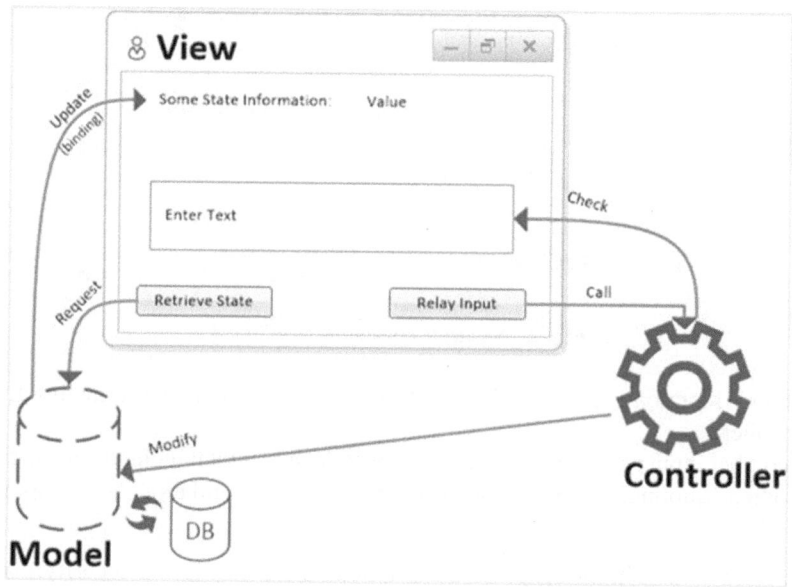

Fig. 1. The Model-View-Controller [9]

Secure software development requires the designer, and developers, to consider the relevance of various secure design principles for the software's context of use. A comprehensive overview of such principles falls outside the scope of this paper. However, in previous work Colesky, Futcher and Van Niekerk [13] demonstrate how many of these principles can be integrated into the MVC pattern. The following discussion provides a brief overview of the proposed secure version of the MVC as shown in Fig. 2.

Figure 2 provides a version of the MVC pattern with the following additional security principles incorporated:

1. Authentication, authorization, access control and trust services were added to the model between the controller and the model. The purpose of these services is to "guard all entrances";
2. A further layer of encipherment, which includes the hashing of passwords, encryption of sensitive data, and hiding of business logic through the preferred use of stored procedures were added to the model;

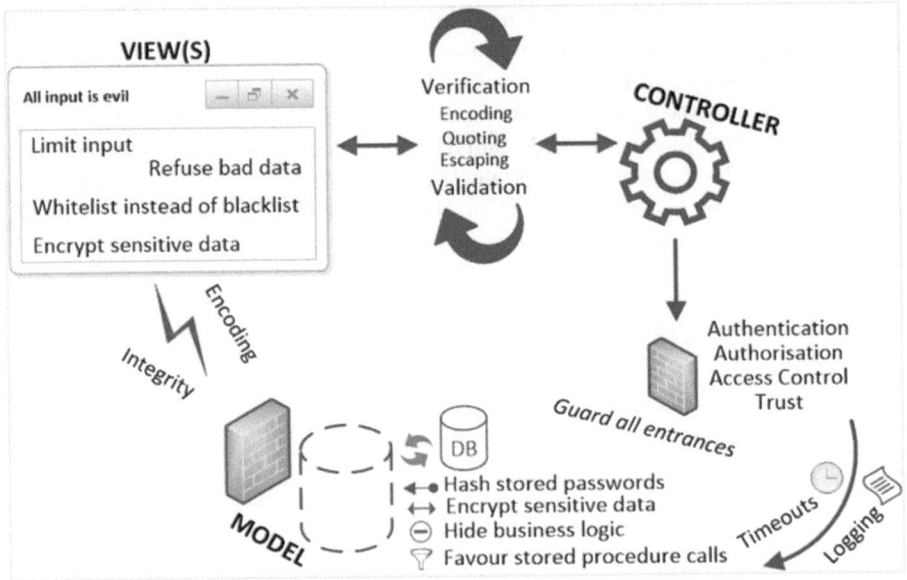

Fig. 2. Security-conscious MVC [13]

3. A notary function is added to log evidence of all transactions originating from the controller;
4. To combat input related risks a layer of mechanisms which include verification, the encoding, quoting, and escaping of characters, and validation of all inputs were added.

The following section discusses the implications of using the security-conscious MVC for teaching secure software design.

5   Discussion

It is important to note that the proposed security-conscious MVC does not prescribe specific technologies for the secure services, but rather provides a specific design context where such services should be sensibly included.

Novice software development students often make mistakes such as placing the code for authentication mechanisms at view level. These mistakes are sometimes further exacerbated by having a username and password visible as unencrypted text within a web page. When developing a web application, many possible technologies could be used for access control and/or encipherment services. The intention of the security conscious MVC pattern is not to dictate a specific technology, but rather to emphasise that there **should** be an access control mechanism, and that this mechanism **should** exist between the Controller and the Model. Access control logic should thus not be exposed at the level of the View. Furthermore, by adding the encipherment layer to the pattern it provides a logical "prompt" for an educator to engage the class regarding what would be sensible to include under these services. For example, *"Should the authentication mechanism make use of encrypted communications?" "What would be an appropriate encryption technology to use for this context?" "Should data exposed by the model be encrypted?"*

One of the first considerations a designer is faced with when designing secure software is how to restrict, or control, access to the underlying data so that only authorised users can view or modify the data. From an access control point of view, the notions of authorisation, authentication, access rights, privileges and trust are of particular importance. Access to data should be given in accordance to the principle of *least privilege*. This principle dictates that an entity should be given access with as few rights as possible [14]; and it also requires that access be permitted for the shortest duration possible [4]. In the authors' experience, discussion of this principle is often done completely out of context and never practiced by software development students.

The use of the security conscious version of the MVC pattern provides a logical prompt for the inclusion of this topic during **every** discussion regarding an n-tier design. By including security considerations as a default into every web application (or similar) development project, students will get substantial exposure to the issues that should be considered and will, hopefully, also get substantial practice during laboratory exercises.

The structure of the presented security-conscious MVC pattern reflects both secure *design principles* and *best practices*. For example, in addition to stimulating discussion regarding the above principle of least privilege, this version of the MVC could also be used to introduce students to the principle of fail-safe defaults, which dictates that the default access granted to a resource should be *none*. Thus, unless access has been granted explicitly to a resource, access to that resource should be denied. In the presented model, this principle is implemented in conjunction with the principle of least privilege via a layered approach. Firstly, the practices of requiring authentication, authorization, and controlling access ensure that only trusted entities are given access to a specific resource. Secondly, because data is encrypted and business logic is hidden, all entities **have to** make use of the access control mechanisms in order to be able to see the underlying data in any form. Thus, should the programmer neglect to verify whether a specific entity should have access, the default behavior would be to present the underlying data in an encrypted format.

According to Martin et al. [15], the top four software vulnerabilities are SQL (Structured Query Language) injection, operating system command injection, buffer overflows and cross-site scripting, respectively. All of these vulnerabilities stem from various forms of malicious input. It is thus vital to include issues related to verification, the encoding, quoting, and escaping of characters, and validation of all inputs consistently during a software design curriculum. The use of this security conscious version of the pattern encourages active discussion regarding these important questions for every n-tier design. By including these topics, both in terms of underlying secure design principles and in terms of secure design best practices, as an integral part of the pattern, educators can ensure that these security services are not seen as an optional add-on, but rather as an essential part of the overall design.

'Education is a very powerful tool in helping to write secure code. By understanding possible threats, programmers can save valuable time and create secure code while

users can rest assured that their information is safer' [16]. The authors believe that the integration of security principles into existing design patterns can be a powerful tool for educators to improve the teaching of secure software design.

6   Limitations and Future Work

The efficacy of this security conscious version of the MVC pattern as a tool to communicate security related concepts to students has not yet been tested. Furthermore, its perceived usefulness for software design educators has not been verified. In this approach, specific implementation details for such a secure MVC pattern was not included. A similar attempt to create a secure MVC pattern, that included more detailed implementation guidance, was presented by Delessy-gassant & Fernandez [17]. However, their approach focused on the inclusion of role based access control into the MVC and was thus considered less generic by the authors who, for the purposes of teaching, specifically aimed to include both security principles and best practices without being too specific regarding implementation. Future work should focus on validating the usefulness of this enhanced version of the pattern for the purpose of teaching secure software design. In addition, the integration of security principles into other software design patterns has not yet been examined.

7   Conclusion

Most aspects of information and cyber security are directly affected by the ability of software developers to produce secure applications. Vulnerabilities caused by poor coding or design practices are a major cause of security breaches. It has become essential for modern software development curricula to address security as an integrated part of the software development process. This paper presents an approach that includes secure software design principles into a commonly used software design pattern. This approach allows the consideration of security principles to form part of the overall design and thus not be relegated as an optional add-on. The authors believe that this approach could play a meaningful role in the teaching of secure software development. Society as a whole can no longer afford to treat security as an afterthought.

References

1. Khan, R.A., Mustafa, K.: Secured requirement specification framework. Am. J. Appl. Sci. **5**(12), 1622–1629 (2008)
2. Burley, D., Bishop, M.: Summit on Education in Secure Software: Final Report. National Science Foundation (2011)
3. Howard, M. (n.d.).: Lessons learned from five years of building more secure software. Accessed 21 Jan 2015, from MSDN Magazine. https://msdn.microsoft.com/en-us/magazine/cc163310.aspx#S1
4. Howard, M., LeBlanc, D.: Writing Secure Code: Practical Strategies and Techniques for Secure Application Coding in a Networked World. Microsoft Press, Redmond (2003)

5. Taylor, B., Azadegan, S.: Threading secure coding principles and risk analysis into the undergraduate computer science and information systems curriculum. In: Information Security Curriculum Development Conference (InfoSecCD), pp. 24–29. ACM, Kennesaw (2006)
6. Heyman, T., Yskout, K., Scandariato, R., Joosen, W.: An analysis of the security patterns landscape. In: 29th International Conference on Software Engineering Workshops (2007)
7. Yoshioka, N., Washizaki, H., Maruyama, K.: A survey on security patterns. Progress in Informatics. Special Issue: The future of software engineering for security and privacy, (5), 35–47 (2008)
8. Barzilay, O., Urquhart, C.: Understanding reuse of software examples: a case study of Prejudice in a community of practice. Inf. Softw. Technol. **56**(12), 1613–1628 (2014)
9. Freeman, E., Freeman, E., Sierra, K., Bates, B.: Head First Design Patterns. O'Reilly Media, Sebastopol (2004)
10. Dooley, J.: Software Development and Professional Practice. Apress, New York (2011)
11. Pieterse, V., Marshall, L.: What is a design pattern? SACLA, 1–25 (2010). http://web.up.ac.za/ecis/SACLA2010PR/SACLA2010/Papers/SACLA030.pdf
12. Syromiatnikov, A., Weyns, D.A.: Journey through the land of model-view-design patterns, WICSA, 2014, 2014 IEEE/IFIP conference on software architecture (WICSA), 2014 IEEE/IFIP conference on software architecture (WICSA), pp. 21–30 (2014)
13. Colesky, M., Futcher, L., Van Niekerk, J.: Design patterns for secure software development: demonstrating security through the MVC pattern. In: 15th Annual Conference on WWW Applications, Cape Town, 10–13 September 2013
14. Meier, J., Mackman, A., Vasireddy, S., Dunner, M., Escamilla, R., Murukan, A.: Improving web application security: threats and countermeasures (p. 919). Microsoft press (2003) http://books.google.com/books?hl=en&lr=&id=Spti0mHhlsUC&oi=fnd&pg=PP2&dq=Improving+Web+Application+Security+Threats+and+Countermeasures&ots=KEfBrKEhQM&sig=mnrDoHKZH93NkQWktonnAw9greE
15. Martin, B., Brown, M., Paller, A., Kirby, D., Christey, S.: 2011 CWE / SANS top 25 most dangerous software errors (2011) http://cwe.mitre.org/top25/archive/2011/2011_cwe_sans_top25.pdf
16. Yu, H., Jones, N., Bullock, G., Yuan, X.Y.: Teaching secure software engineering: writing secure code. In: 2011 7th Central and Eastern European Software Engineering Conference, CEE-SECR 2011, pp. 1–5 (2011)
17. Delessy-gassant, N., Fernandez, E.B.: The secure MVC pattern. In: 1st LACCEI International Symposium on Software Architecture and Patterns, (pp. 1–6). Panama, Panama City (2012)

Tools and Applications
for Teaching

Learn to Spot Phishing URLs
with the Android NoPhish App

Gamze Canova, Melanie Volkamer$^{(\boxtimes)}$, Clemens Bergmann, Roland Borza,
Benjamin Reinheimer, Simon Stockhardt, and Ralf Tenberg

Center for Advanced Security Research Darmstadt (CASED),
Technische Universität Darmstadt, Darmstadt, Germany
{Gamze.Canova,Clemens.Bergmann,Roland.Borza,Benjamin.Reinheimer,
Ralf.Tenberg,Melanie.Volkamer,Simon.Stockhardt}@cased.de

Abstract. Phishing is a münich issue in today's Internet. It can have
financial or personal consequences. Attacks continue to become more and
more sophisticated and the advanced ones (including spear phishing)
can only be detected if people carefully check URLs – be it in messages
or in the address bar of the web browser. We developed a game-based
smartphone app – *NoPhish* – to educate people in accessing, parsing and
checking URLs; i.e. enabling them to distinguish between trustworthy
and non-trustworthy messages and websites. Throughout several levels
of the game information is provided and phishing detection is exercised
in a playful manner. Several learning principles were applied and the
interfaces and texts were developed in a user-centered design.

1 Introduction

The financial benefit of phishing [1] is an incentive for phishers to keep luring victims into disclosing their sensitive information. The anti-phishing working group
registered more than 120.000 unique phishing attacks in the first half of 2014,
i.e. more than 120.000 impersonated websites [2]. Furthermore, they report that
the average up-time of phishing websites was 32 h and 32 min. During this time
potential victims have to be self-reliant, i.e. they have to check the URL in order to
know whether the destination is trustworthy. People could be supported by tools
such as the Netcraft Extension [3]. However, such tools can never provide 100 %
accuracy [4]. Therefore, the tools' checks need to be complemented by humans
checking the URLs. Yet, many people lack the required knowledge to properly
check URLs [5,6] and assess the trustworthiness of a given website. Some people
are even not aware of faked messages and websites at all and, thus, are not aware
that they should check URLs before providing sensitive information [5,7].

Several solutions have been proposed to address the problem of lacking knowledge e.g. tutorials or guides [8,9], quizzes [10,11] and games [4,12]. Tutorials are
read-intensive if they cover all the different channels (such as email, SMS, QR
codes, instant messaging, and social media) and URL spoofing tricks phishers
exploit. The quizzes we are aware of do – if at all – indirectly educate people
based on the feedback whether given answers are correct or incorrect; i.e. they

© IFIP International Federation for Information Processing 2015
M. Bishop et al. (Eds.): WISE9, IFIP AICT 453, pp. 87–100, 2015.
DOI: 10.1007/978-3-319-18500-2_8

do not explain why answers are correct/incorrect. In addition, they do not cover all different channels and tricks phishers exploit. The game Anti-Phishing Phyllis [12] only focuses on the email channel. Anti-Phishing Phil 1 and 2 [4,13] are already rather advanced in terms of different URL spoofing tricks; but can still be improved by including awareness aspects, addressing different channels, explaining the structure of a URL more precisely, addressing more categories of URL spoofing tricks, and providing knowledge about HTTPS.

Our goal[1] was to develop a new game – *NoPhish* – an anti-phishing education app that addresses these issues to provide more sophisticated knowledge on how to properly check URLs – be it in messages or in the address bar of the web browser. We opted for an Android smartphone app since in particular smartphone users are much more likely to access phishing websites than desktop users [15]. The detection of phishing on mobile browsers is complicated because in many cases address bars disappear and even if shown only parts of the URL are visible. Furthermore, a smartphone app provides the opportunity of casual gameplay and thus, compared to desktop solutions, more flexibility and time-independence. Thanks to the Google Play Game Services it is also possible for users to compare their performance with others. This adds a supplementary challenge and a motivational aspect, both key characteristics of gameplay and therefore successful learning. Furthermore, *NoPhish* integrates a number of learning principles recommended by literature.

2 Preliminary Considerations

2.1 Required Skills

Earlier phishing attacks could be detected by checking messages and websites for spelling and grammar mistakes or for design flaws. But since phishing attacks get more advanced, the URL is the only reliable indicator for the authenticity and trustworthiness of messages and websites (note, assuming a non-compromised system). Correspondingly, the following skills are required to successfully protect against phishing:

- Being aware that messages, links and websites can be easily impersonated;
- Knowing that the URL is a reliable indicator for the authenticity and trustworthiness of a website rather than a website's content;
- Knowing how to access and view entire URL;
- Knowing how to parse the URL properly;
- Knowing different URL spoofing tricks;
- Knowing the importance of HTTPS when entering sensitive data.

2.2 Target Group

With *NoPhish*, we address in particular people who lack knowledge regarding all the aspects listed in Sect. 2.1; but people who use the Internet frequently.

---

[1] Note, a summary of this paper is available at [14].

We assume that *NoPhish* users have a general interest in learning to protect themselves (as they decided to install the app). Furthermore, our target group are Germans[2].

2.3   Learning Focus

URLs can either be checked using the URL preview function (cf. Fig. 1) provided by several email clients and mobile browsers or directly in the mobile browser's address bar. We decided to educate people how to check URLs in the address bar for the following reasons: First, not all applications provide such a preview function, e.g. Android's (e.g. version 4.2) standard email client (e.g. version 4.4.2) does not provide such a preview function. Second, well-crafted URLs can still deceive users since the preview URLs are cropped in case they are too long (cf. Fig. 1). We are aware that this decision comes with the disadvantage that users might fall for an attack by clicking on a link already, e.g. they could download malicious software. This issue is addressed by *NoPhish* in the final remarks (cf. Sect. 3.5).

Fig. 1. Screenshot - URL preview function

2.4   Categorization of URL Spoofing Tricks

Phishers apply several URL spoofing tricks. Different tricks should be explained in different levels of *NoPhish*. There are several approaches to categorize URL spoofing tricks [4,6,16]. We propose to use a different categorization; one that is based on the difficulty to detect the corresponding spoofing trick. Such a categorization is most appropriate for the later leveling. Correspondingly, we identified the following categories (note, the examples are taken from PhishTank):

(a) *IP Address URL without Brand:* Sometimes phishers do not even bother registering any domain at all. In this spoofing trick, the host area of the URL contains an IP address while the path part does not contain the brand name, e.g. http://5.178.64.164/securetoimpersonatePayPal.

---

[2] Note, this has an impact on the language as well as on the selected URLs and the design of the app.

(b) *Random/Unrelated/Trustworthy Domain, without Brand:* This trick uses random/unrelated or trustworthy names or strings as domain name[3] and does not include the brand name of the targeted website in any other part of the URL. E.g. http://www.szuhsa.fr/login.html, http://www.weather.com/login.html or https://secure-payment.com to impersonate PayPal.

(c) *Random/Unrelated/Trustworthy Domain, with Brand in Subdomain:* A phisher can include the brand name into the subdomain of a URL in combination with a random/unrelated/trustworthy domain name, e.g. http://paypal.mark-chippy.com/account-setup/ or http://www.amazon.account.com/.

(d) *Random/Unrelated/Trustworthy/IP Domain, with Brand in Path:* A phisher can include the brand name into the path part of a URL in combination with a random/unrelated/trustworthy domain name, e.g. http://online-payment.com/www.paypal.com/. This attack can also happen in combination with an IP address URL, e.g. http://5.178.64.164/paypal.

(e) *Derivated Domains:* A phisher can register a modification of the original domain. In this case the modified domain contains the brand name in some form, e.g. facebook-login.com can be registered in order to impersonate facebook.com.

(f) *Introducing Typos:* Phishers can register domains which resemble the targeted domain, but have a typo, e.g. the phisher can register micosoft.com to impersonte micosoft.com. One special case of the typo is swapping letters in the original domain name, e.g. micosoft.com to impersonate microsoft.com.

(g) *Replacing Character(s):* A phisher can also exploit character resemblance, i.e. the phisher can register domains where characters are replaced by other similar characters, e.g. https://www.arnazon.com.

There are some more URL spoofing tricks which either cannot be recognized by the human eye (e.g. homograph attacks [17]) or are irrelevant for our setting because they are redirected URLs such as tiny URLs [18] or cloaked URLs [19]. After succefully completing the last level of the game, some general remarks on these issues are provided to the users (cf. Sect. 3.5).

2.5 Learning Principles

This section explains the principles of learning according to [20,21] which are essential for increased learning performance:

Readiness: The principle of readiness states that motivation is crucial for effective learning. Note, due to the definition of the target group we assume that *NoPhish* users entail readiness.

Exercise: The principle of exercise is composed of two aspects: First, training and repetition help increase learning. Second, feedback is crucial for good learning performance. Ideally, these two aspects are applied in combination.

---

[3] Note, that we refer to the first- and second-level domain of a URL as domain.

Effect: The principle of effect states that people who associate their learning with positive feelings, e.g. early successes, learn more and better while on the other hand, negative feelings can decrease the learning performance. Correspondingly, enabling early success and maintaining people's motivation with positive feedback is crucial for successful learning.

Intensity: The principle of intensity states that learning is encouraged by things that are more intense. E.g. people are likely to learn more from an exciting and enthusiastic teacher than from a boring and monotone one or from a text book.

Primacy: The principle of primacy states that the first thing people learn makes the strongest impression; i.e. it should be started with important content.

2.6   Gamification

The following game elements are used in most modern games [22,23] and are important for a good game experience:

Lives: An inherent element of a game is the possibility of losing it. If users are not able to lose a game they have no incentive to win it or play it. At the same time, one does not want the user to lose the game directly as the result of one minor mistake. Therefore, most games have some kind of "you have N tries"-element, which is commonly referred to as lives.

Levels: Leveling serves multiple purposes: First, it is important for the users to get a feeling for the progress they make. Second, it provides fixed points in the game from where they can restart or pause and continue the game later on. Finally, it enables to increase the difficulty of the game with increasing levels.

Achievements: Achievements are special elements of a game that users can unlock if they, e.g. find a special object or if they play a certain level exceptionally well. This is in particular for people who are willing to invest a lot of time in a specific level in order to finish it perfectly or to find every hidden secret in it.

Leaderboards: A leaderboard is an area where a user can compare the own progress in the game with the one of other users. The comparison with others motivates people to improve skills relevant for the game resulting in better performance.

2.7   User-Centered Design

The design and implementation of a user friendly and understandable app as described by Abras et al. [24] is achieved by giving extensive attention to the users' needs and wants as early as possible.

3   Game Design

This section elaborates on the game design and explains how the identified aspects of Sect. 2 are addressed.

3.1   Initial Survey

Before elaborating on the app design and implementation we inteded to get an idea of the users' preferences with regard to an anti-phishing education app. Thus, we ran an initial user survey where we asked users whether they would prefer a rather neutral game or a comic style education game with e.g. a fish as main character. The results of our survey confirmed previous findings by Volkamer et al. [25] that for a German audience (adults at least) a rather neutral game-based approach would be best accepted.

3.2   Learning Content per Part

The app entails two introductory parts, the game with nine levels, and a final remarks part. Table 1 shows the link between the skills to properly judge on the trustworthiness of websites (cf. Sect. 2.1) and the different parts of *NoPhish*.

Table 1. Skills – levels – assignment

Taught Skill	Covered in
Awareness of fake messages, links and websites	Intro Part 1
Access and view entire URL	Intro Part 2
URL as a reliable indicator for phishing attacks	Intro Part 2
Proper URL parsing	Level 1
Different URL spoofing tricks (cf. Section 2.4)	Levels 2-8
a) IP address, no brand	Level 2
b) Random/unrelated/trustworthy domain, no brand	Level 3
c) Random/unrelated/trustworthy domain, brand in subdomain	Level 4
d) Random/unrelated/trustworthy/IP domain, brand in path	Level 5
e) Derivated domains	Level 6
f) Introducing typos	Level 7
g) Replacing character(s)	Level 8
HTTPS for entering sensitive data	Level 9

3.3   Introduction Parts

After a short introduction to the problem of phishing and its consequences, *NoPhish* starts with two introductory parts. The *awareness of spoofed messages, links, and websites* can be best addressed by actually sending corresponding messages and *access and view entire URL* can be best exercised in the mobile browser. Thus, these two parts are seperated from the actual levels of the game.

Part 1 - Awareness of Spoofed Messages, Links, and Websites: First, users are made aware of how simple it is to spoof messages, e.g. emails [26]. This is done by enabling them to send themselves with the *NoPhish* app an email from a sender address they provide in a corresponding form; and with a content they provide there as well. After submitting the form, *NoPhish* requests the users to check their email inbox. The received email contains information that this email was sent by *NoPhish* and that users should check the "from field" to notice that this is actually the email they prepared. Furthermore, the email contains a link with the displayed text "https://www.google.de/" and users are asked to follow the link. Clicking on this link redirects the users back to the app. Thereby, users learn by experience that they should not trust displayed link texts. Back in the app some further information is provided, e.g. that website spoofing is simple as well. Finally, the user is informed that this kind of forgery is not only possible with emails, but also with other forms of communication, such as social networks, SMS or instant messaging systems.

Part 2 - Access Address Bar and View Entire URL: This part teaches the users how to access and view the entire URL in the mobile browser. In detail, the users are told (1) that they need to scroll up the entire website to make the generally hidden address bar reappear; and (2) that they need to tap the text field of the address bar and scroll to the left in order to view the entire URL. The explanations how to do so are supported with corresponding screenshots.

Due to the learning principle of *exercise* (cf. Sect. 2.5) after the explanations an exercise follows. Here, users are required to access the URL of a website they are forwarded to by *NoPhish*. Note, forwarding happens in a way that users first have to scroll up. On top of the page, there is a text field, where they are asked to enter the last four characters of the URL. Then, they are asked to identify the first word of the URL (check one out of four provided possibilities). Once submitted the app checks the users' answers and can thereby ensure that they managed to access and view the entire URL. The users are forwarded to *NoPhish* as soon as they successfully complete the exercise. At the end of the exercise the users are told that URLs are the only reliable indicator for phishing. They also learn that they should always access the URL just as learned and that all other displayed links might be spoofed (by referring to the previous part). This part closes by explaining that URLs need to be carefully checked and that they learn how to do so throughout the coming parts of the app.

3.4   Gaming Part

The gaming part is split into nine levels with increasing difficulty. Each level consists of two parts: an introductory block and the actual exercise. For the introduction of URL spoofing tricks the introductory block consists of a reminder[4],

---

[4] Note, this reminder is not shown if the user immediately starts off the new level after having successfully completed the last one but only if some time passed since the user played previous levels.

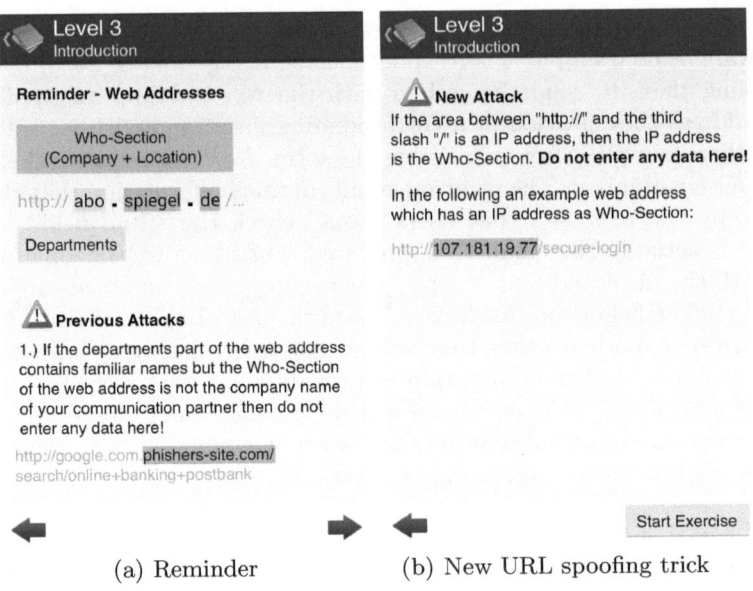

(a) Reminder   (b) New URL spoofing trick

Fig. 2. Example introductory block

which provides a summary of previous levels (cf. Fig. 2(a)) and the introduction of a new URL spoofing trick (cf. Fig. 2(b)).

The exercise is designed in a playful manner, i.e. users start with three lives, represented by hearts, and can collect points for correct answers and lose points and lives for wrong ones.

Users receive direct feedback on their decision. If the given answer is correct the users are rewarded by gaining points and a smiley face. This is relevant for the increase of positive feelings (cf. learning principle of *effect* in Sect. 2.5). If the answer is wrong the users lose points and a life. The users are immediately told why their answer was wrong. The next level is achieved if and only if a predefined amount of phishing and legitimate URLs have correctly been identified.

To simulate the "behavior" of the address bar in mobile browsers, the entire URL as such is not displayed but only parts of it. The user needs to scroll to the start of the URL in order to decide about the legitimacy of the displayed URL.

By practicing the learnt content and providing direct feedback we address the principle of *exercise* (cf. Sect. 2.5). Note, by making use of *levels* and *lives* two of the four gamification elements are already addressed (cf. Sect. 2.6). The elements *achievements* and *leadersboards* are realized by means of Google Play Game Services. Finally, *NoPhish* by nature provides intensity (cf. learning principle of *intensity* in Sect. 2.5) as it is a game.

Level 1 - Structure of a URL: It is essential for people to achieve the capability of parsing a URL properly before learning different URL spoofng tricks. Especially the identification of the domain (first- and second-level domain) in a given URL is a key aspect which needs to be covered extensively. Therefore, the users start learning to identify the domain of a URL in level 1. To explain the different parts, we do not use technical terms such as URL, domain, subdomain, protocol and only provide details users need to know to successfully detect phishing URLs. The focus of this level is the domain, the *Who-Section* as we refer to it in NoPhish. During the exercise the users are asked to tap on the *Who-Section*.

Levels 2–8 - URL Spoofing Tricks: In levels 2–8, the various URL spoofing tricks (cf. Sect. 2.4) are addressed. In level 2, we also explain IP addresses by using the analogy of house addresses (with street names and numbers).

During the exercises, URLs together with the name of the website the users are supposed to visit are displayed (cf. Fig. 3(a)). Users are asked to decide whether they are legitimate or phishing ones. Note, that in all levels both, HTTP and HTTPS URLs are displayed to the user, i.e. legitimate as well as phishing URLs can use HTTPS. This way, we prevent users from deciding based on the protocol.

When the users correctly identify a phishing URL, *NoPhish* asks them to tap on the *Who-Section* (cf. Fig. 3(b)). This way, we aspire to ensure that they understood where to look at and did not just guess the answer. Depending on the user performance the frequency of asking to tap on the *Who-Section* decreases or increases.

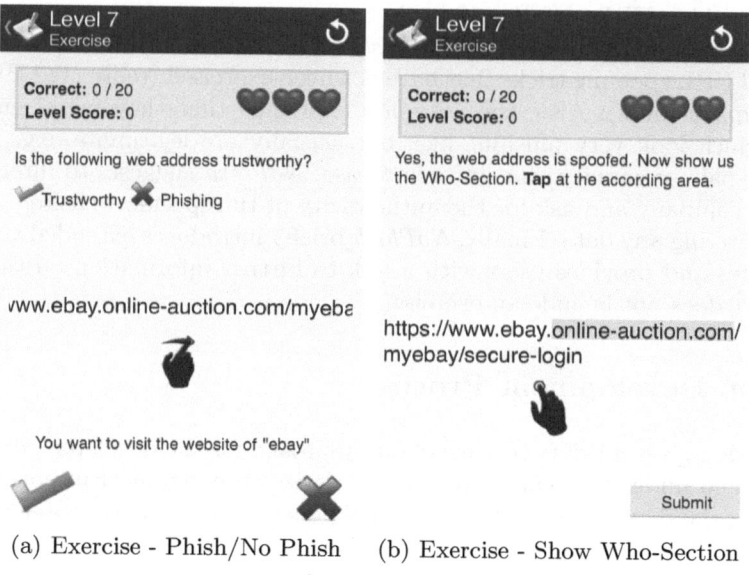

(a) Exercise - Phish/No Phish   (b) Exercise - Show Who-Section

Fig. 3. Example exercise screenshots

Note, in level n the number of URLs that need to be properly judged is $6 + 2 * (n + 1)$. The learning principle of *repetition* (cf. Sect. 2.5) is applied as each URL spoofing trick introduced in level n is tested in the exercises of later levels, too. About half of the phishing URLs (more precisely $\lfloor (6 + 2 * (n + 1))/4 \rfloor$ in level

n) are repetitions[5] from previous levels. The first level that contains repetitions is level 3 because level 2 introduces the first URL spoofing trick.

Level 9 - HTTPS: In this level, we introduce the difference between HTTP and HTTPS. We explain, that HTTPS represents the higher security level and that this means (1) that the conversation cannot be eavesdropped by someone having access to the network and (2) that the communication partner indicated in the *Who-Section* proved his/her identity to a trusted authority if no warning is shown in the browser.

Furthermore, we tell users that there exist many legitimate websites without HTTPS (by default). We advice to try to switch to HTTPS. We explain the consequences if sensitive information is entered on a website without HTTPS (while assuming that the domain name is authentic). This level also includes an exercise. However, the question is changed. The users are asked whether they would provide sensitive information on the website. Thus, the users need to check whether a URL provides HTTPS and whether the domain name of the URL is spoofed or not.

3.5   Final Remarks Part

When the users reach the final remarks part they are well prepared for the detection of phishing URLs (cf. Sect. 2.1). Yet, there are some special cases the users are made aware of in this part of *NoPhish*. E.g. users are informed about further potential URL spoofing tricks that have not been exercised (redirected URLs and homograph attacks). Also, the users are explained that they might encounter URLs which look very phishing-like, but actually are legitimate, e.g. https:// www.paypal-community.com. In such a case, *NoPhish* suggests to directly contact the company and ask for the authenticity of the specific website, i.e. URL, before entering any data. Finally, *NoPhish* briefly introduces extended validation certificates and provides users with a link to further information on this topic. This part does not include an exercise.

4   App Development Process

This section gives a brief overview of our approach for the development of a user friendly and understandable app and summarizes the two most important steps regarding the development process – URL generation and user-centered design.

4.1   URL Generation

We generate phishing URLs by applying corresponding URL spoofing tricks to legitimate URLs. For the legitimate URLs 30 of the top 100 Alexa ranked domains (for Germany) were collected. The corresponding URLs have no path

---

[5] Repetition means that the URL spoofing trick is repeated not the specific URLs.

or subdomain, e.g. google.com. In order to also provide *NoPhish* users with longer URLs, we visited each of these websites, navigated through them and additionally picked three URLs for each domain, two long and one short URL. Thus, for each domain, a total of four URLs was added to the set of legitimate URLs. This set contains URLs with and without HTTPS.

For each URL to be displayed it is randomly decided which of the legitimate URLs is used. Then, it is randomly decided whether to show a legitimate or a phishing one based on the setting for the corresponding level. For the phishing URLs the corresponding URL spoofing trick is applied.

4.2   Applied User-Centered Design Approaches

In addition to the initial survey, we involved potential users of *NoPhish* in the following ways: we iteratively built, tested, and improved mock ups (while focusing on the first three levels as the app flow does not significantly change from this level on). For instance, according to comments of participants, we simplified and clarified the descriptions on how to access the address bar. We also reduced the text per page in general. The texts for all levels were reviewed by two German language experts (who are no security experts).

The next step was a user study, where we decided to go for the low cost method of guerilla user testing [27]; i.e. participants reading the app texts while thinking aloud. We included a little exercise in order to assess whether the users comprehended the texts or not, i.e. for each introduced URL spoofing trick we included a small list of URLs on which the users had to decide whether they were phishing URLs or not. Finally, the users were asked to provide their general impression. The received feedback was integrated.

In addition, we applied a statistical method – once we improved the text – in order to assess the legibility of our texts. Corresponding tools [28–30] take a regular text as their input and return a legibility index as their output. The average index value of the three tools for the entire text used in the app is 62. Given a scale from 0 to 100, where an index of up to 30 indicates an academic level and 90 and above is considered easy to understand, an index of 62 is considered as reasonably comprehensive for teenagers [31]. Regarding our target group, this result is reasonable. However, it is something we have in mind for later user tests to evaluate.

5   Related Work

Section 1 already gives an overview of related work in anti-phishing education. Here, we especially elaborate on Anti-Phishing Phil 1 and 2 [4,13], as these games resemble *NoPhish* the most of all the anti-phishing education approaches.

Anti-Phishing Phil 2 uses a diver as main character (while Anti-Phishing Phil 1 uses a fish). A major improvement compared to Anti-Phishing Phil 1 is that the game emphasizes the importance of the domain. E.g. the users are asked to mark the part of a URL which indicates phishing. This is an aspect we included to *NoPhish*. Furthermore, the information texts are generally improved and extended to be more precise.

The design of Anti-Phishing Phil 2 as such could not be applied for our context due to the results of our initial survey. However, we carefully analyzed the structure and the educated content to decide what could be adapted and what we wanted to modify or improve: The provided information, is often not precise enough and sometimes even inconsistent. In one information text the host is introduced as the part between "http://" and the first "/" and the domain is right before the first "/". In another information text the domain is addressed by referring to the right hand side of the host area, which could be either only the top level domain or could also include subdomains. In addition, Anti-Phishing Phil 2 covers only four URL spoofing tricks (similar to Anti-Phishing Phil 1): subdomain tricks, IP addresses, domains with hyphens (part of derivated domain names) and replacing character(s).

The users are asked to decide on only three URLs per level which seems not to be enough in order to internalize the learnt content according to the principle of *exercise*. Also, URL spoofing tricks from previous levels are not repeated which is essential for good learning performance according to the learning principle of *exercise*. Finally, the difference between HTTP and HTTPS is not addressed as well as the contents of introduction parts 1 and 2 of *NoPhish*.

6   Conclusion and Future Work

In the scope of this work, we have designed and implemented an anti-phishing education app – *NoPhish* – in a user-centered design approach. In a playful manner, users obtain valuable information on how to detect phishing URLs, in particular on a smartphone. The detection of phishing URLs is realized as a game, where the user can win or lose points or lives.

We integrated learning principles and diverse gamification elements recommended in literature. In order to provide levels, with increasing difficulty to detect phishing URLs, we proposed a new categorization of URL spoofing tricks which we then explain in the different levels.

The app is divided into two main parts: the security awareness and the educational part. In the security awareness part the user is shown how simple it is to spoof emails and links by sending themselves a spoofed email with a spoofed link. In the educational part the user is taught how to access the URL and how to detect phishing URLs.

We already conducted a user study including a retention study which showed very promising results [14]. In future, we also plan to assess how such an education app can best be distributed. An idea would be to utilize embedded learning [32] where simulated phishing emails are sent to users. Whenever users fall for such an email they could be proposed to download the education app. We also plan to extend the target group and consider kids and youth.

Acknowledgements. This work was supported by CASED and EC SPRIDE.

References

1. Ramzan, Z.: Phishing attacks and countermeasures. In: Stavroulakis, P., Stamp, M. (eds.) Handbook of Information and Communication Security, pp. 433–448. Springer, Heidelberg (2010)
2. Aaron, G., Rasmussen, R., Routt, A.: Global Phishing Survey: Trends and Domain Name Use in 1h2014. Anti-Phishing Working Group (APWG), Lexington (2014)
3. Netcraft: Netcraft extension. http://toolbar.netcraft.com. Accessed 05 June 2014
4. Sheng, S., Magnien, B., Kumaraguru, P., Acquisti, A., Cranor, L.F., Hong, J., Nunge, E.: Anti-phishing phil: the design and evaluation of a game that teaches people not to fall for phish. In: Proceedings of the 3rd Symposium on Usable Privacy and Security, SOUPS 2007, pp. 88–99. ACM, New York (2007)
5. Dhamija, R., Tygar, J.D., Hearst, M.: Why phishing works. In: Proceedings of the SIGCHI Conference on Human Factors in Computing Systems, pp. 581–590. ACM (2006)
6. Lin, E., Greenberg, S., Trotter, E., Ma, D., Aycock, J.: Does domain highlighting help people identify phishing sites? In: Proceedings of the SIGCHI Conference on Human Factors in Computing Systems, pp. 2075–2084. ACM (2011)
7. Li, T., Han, F., Ding, S., Chen, Z.: Larx: large-scale anti-phishing by retrospective data-exploring based on a cloud computing platform. In: 2011 Proceedings of 20th International Conference on Computer Communications and Networks (ICCCN), pp. 1–5. IEEE (2011)
8. Bundesamt für Sicherheit in der Informationstechnik: Phishing: Gefährliche umleitung für ihre passwörter. https://www.bsi-fuer-buerger.de/BSIFB/DE/GefahrenImNetz/Phishing/phishing_node.html. Accessed 26 May 2014
9. OnGuardOnline.gov: Phishing. http://www.onguardonline.gov/phishing. Accessed 26 May 2014
10. Online, S.S.: Race to stay safe. https://www.staysecureonline.com/staying-safe-online. Accessed 26 May 2014
11. SonicWALL: Sonicwall phishing iq test. http://www.sonicwall.com/furl/phishing. Accessed 26 May 2014
12. Wombat Security Technologies: Anti-phishing phyllis. http://www.wombatsecurity.com/antiphishingphyllis. Accessed 26 May 2014
13. Aleven, V., Chan, S.H., Moore, A., Sung, A.: Anti-phishing phil v2.0. http://jackieweber.net/Projects/phil.html. Accessed 05 June 2014
14. Canova, G., Volkamer, M., Bergmann, C., Borza, R.: NoPhish: an anti-phishing education app. In: Mauw, S., Jensen, C.D. (eds.) STM 2014. LNCS, vol. 8743, pp. 188–192. Springer, Heidelberg (2014)
15. Boodaei, M.: Mobile users three times more vulnerable to phishing attacks (2011). http://www.trusteer.com/blog/mobile-users-three-times-more-vulnerable-to-phishing-attacks. Accessed 28 May 2014
16. Garera, S., Provos, N., Chew, M., Rubin, A.D.: A framework for detection and measurement of phishing attacks. In: Proceedings of the 2007 ACM Workshop on Recurring Malcode, pp. 1–8. ACM (2007)
17. Gabrilovich, E., Gontmakher, A.: The homograph attack. Commun. ACM **45**(2), 128 (2002)
18. Larkin, E.: Spot the tiny phishing trick (2009). http://www.pcworld.com/article/161232/tinyphish.html. Accessed 26 May 2014
19. Alnajim, A.: Fighting internet fraud: anti-phishing effectiveness for phishing websites detection. Ph.D. thesis, Durham University (2009)

20. Thorndike, E.L.: The Fundamentals of Learning. Teachers College Bureau of Publications, New York (1932)
21. Murphy, C.: Why games work and the science of learning. In: Interservice, Interagency Training, Simulations, and Education Conference (2011)
22. Badgeville: Game mechanics. http://badgeville.com/wiki/Game_Mechanics. Accessed 10 June 2014
23. Siering, G.: Gamification: using game-like elements to motivate and engage students (2012). citl.indiana.edu/news/newsStories/dir-mar2012.php. Accessed 10 June 2014
24. Abras, C., Maloney-krichmar, D., Preece, J.: User-centered design. In: Bainbridge, W. (ed.) Encyclopedia of Human-Computer Interaction. Sage Publications, Thousand Oaks (2004)
25. Volkamer, M., Stockhardt, S., Bartsch, S., Kauer, M.: Adopting the CMU/APWG anti-phishing landing page idea for germany. In: 2013 Third Workshop on Socio-Technical Aspects in Security and Trust (STAST), pp. 46–52. IEEE (2013)
26. Avoine, G., Junod, P., Oechslin, P.: Computer System Security: Basic Concepts and Solved Exercises. EPFL Press, Lausanne (2004)
27. Simon, D.P.: The art of guerilla usability testing (2013). http://www.uxbooth.com/articles/the-art-of-guerilla-usability-testing/. Accessed 26 May 2014
28. Stilversprechend: Stilversprechend. http://stilversprechend.de/index.html. Accessed 26 May 2014
29. Leicht Lesbar: Testen sie ihren text. http://leichtlesbar.ch/html. Accessed 26 May 2014
30. Schöll, P.: Flesch-index berechnen. http://www.fleschindex.de. Accessed 26 May 2014
31. Amstad, T.: Wie verständlich sind unsere Zeitungen?. Abhandlung: Philosophische Fakultät I, 1977. Studenten-Schreib-Service, Zürich (1978)
32. Jansson, K., von Solms, R.: Simulating malicious emails to educate end users on-demand. In: 2011 3rd Symposium on Web Society (SWS), pp. 74–80 (2011)

An Innovative Approach in Digital Forensic Education and Training

Primož Cigoj[1,2] and Borka Jerman Blažič[2(✉)]

[1] Jožef Stefan International Postgraduate School,
Jamova Cesta 39, 1000 Ljubljana, Slovenia
[2] Laboratory for Open Systems and Networks, Jozef Stefan Institute,
Jamova Cesta 39, 1000 Ljubljana, Slovenia
{primoz,borka}@e5.ijs.si

Abstract. This paper present a novel approach to education in the area of digital forensics based on a multi-platform cloud-computer infrastructure and an innovative computer based tool. The paper presents the tool and describe the different levels of college and university education where the tool is introduced. The tool provides multi-level training that is initiated with the educational levels of the exercises and the content applied. The assessment of the achieved results is provided by the tool at the end of the training session.

Keywords: Digital forensic · Training environment · Education · Cloud computing · Forensic tool

1 Introduction

E-learning has now been around for more than 10 years. During this time it has changed from being a radical idea, the effectiveness of which was yet to be proven, to something that is now widely regarded as mainstream in modern education. It is also considered as being the core of numerous business plans and services offered by many colleges and universities [1]. Currently, e-learning tends to take the form of online courses. These courses differ in terms of their technology and content, ranging from the resources distributed by MIT's OpenCourseWare project [2] to the design of learning materials offered by colleges and universities from all around the world, acting as the basic unit for the organization of curriculums. The dominant learning technology employed for the management of e-learning is a type of system that organizes, delivers the online courses, and then follows the accomplishments of the learning objectives; it is called the Learning Management System (LMS). This piece of software, which is usually part of the university's network infrastructure, has become almost ubiquitous in most of the known e-learning environments. Other recent technologies, for example, cloud-computing platforms, are not yet being heavily exploited in the area of e-learning training. This is especially the case for education in the area of digital forensic engineering, which is a field associated with cyber security and the fight against cybercrime and cyber terrorism. These fields are very specific and require intelligent, adaptable approaches that respond to user requirements, coming mainly from officers and members of LEAs (law-enforcement agencies), or private investigators, prosecutors and other cybercrime

M. Bishop et al. (Eds.): WISE9, IFIP AICT 453, pp. 101–110, 2015.
DOI: 10.1007/978-3-319-18500-2_9

combatants. Criminal justice education, where digital forensic engineering belongs, is still conducted in a very traditional manner, especially when it comes to capturing digital forensic evidence and its subsequent analysis. The training environment for computer forensics and the methods for fighting cybercrime in most traditional institutions are carried out mainly as a static type of training and closely follow traditional matters and approaches in the criminal justice curriculum. The practical exercises and the challenges presented to the students are usually refreshed slowly [3–5]. The exercises that accompany the curriculum are mainly carried out in a class studying classic examples. The practical work is focused on solving a task: "find the flag", and the flag to be found is always at the same location as where the training takes place. In a real-life situation, digital investigators are faced with much more complex tasks, where they are forced to use a wide range of methods to solve the problem [6].

In this paper we describe a novel approach to educating and training in the area of digital forensic engineering. The training is based on the use of a dynamic tool developed within the E-Forensics Educational Community that acts within the D-FET project consortium (Digital Forensic Education and Training project). The tool is installed and offered over the cloud-based infrastructure of the D-FET project [7]. Cloud computing introduces an efficient mechanism for a wide range of services that offer real-life environments in the area of cybersecurity and digital forensics, which is not being sufficiently well exploited for on-line education. The cloud-based infrastructure enables the construction of on-dynamic e-learning systems and tools, making this training very close to reality and to real-life situations [8]. The DFET project is funded within the EU's ISEC program [9] and the main objective is the development of an innovative educational approach in the area of digital forensics.

The paper is organized as follows: the next section introduces the cloud-based infrastructure and the basic features of the EduFors tool. The section that follows describes the technical details of the tool and the educational approach applied during the training process. The collected experiences of the performed training and the received feedback are presented in the fourth section, which is followed by a brief discussion and concluding remarks.

2   The D-FET Cloud-Computing Training Environment

The D-FET project is a training environment that consists of a virtual cloud-based platform that enables the sharing of courses and the use of laboratory training material. The training environment is built up from virtual machines that are generated to an extent that depends on the number of enrolled trainees, meaning that the number of virtual machines is sufficient for the requirements of the training. They can be accessed remotely. The training environment is dynamic and follows the evolving nature of the analytical cybercrime methods and approaches, as well as the technology development of cyberspace. The D-FET training environment caters for a range of educational levels, enabling education for Information and Communications Technology (ICT) students and as well as for law-enforcement professionals. Currently, the cloud infrastructure is owned and shared by the institutions of the participating countries (Slovenia, UK, Ireland, and Sweden).

Figure 1 outlines the generalised training infrastructure and the approach used in creating real-life-based instances of cybercrime attacks or fraud, where an instructor has the possibility to generate an active instance for the training challenge, such as one related to finding data associated with an act of crime on a PC or on a smartphone. These active instances are generally based on known criminal use cases, such as the investigation of a computer for financial fraud, or a denial of service, where an investigation must create an evidence bag and handle the evidence correctly according to the legislative rules, making it intelligible for use in a court. The cloud platform contains an incorporated educational tool known as EduFors, which is designed to provide several cyber forensics images, as instances originating from an attacked operating system or network server.

Using this tool, multiple instances across the network are created and the challenge presented to the trainee is to collect the evidence from the criminal attack across a

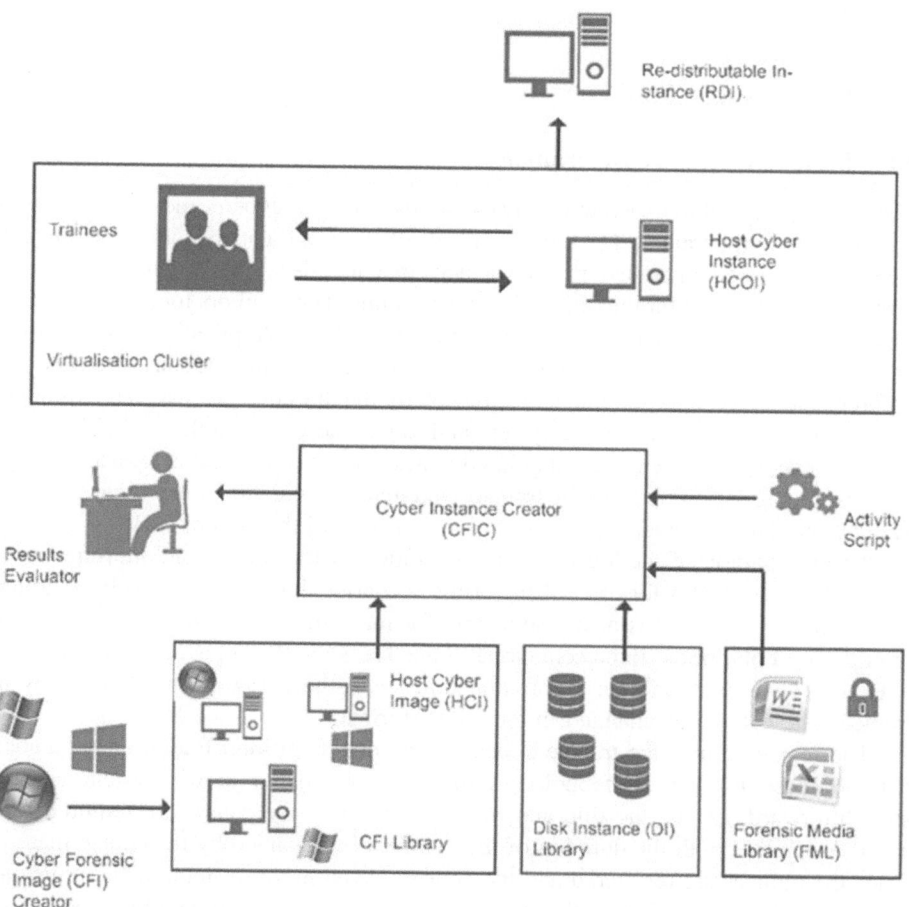

Fig. 1. The general training infrastructure

number of network-connected devices. The tool then adds the required disk instances for selected scenarios of different types of criminal act and prepares them to be analysed by a digital forensic tool, such as the X-Ways software packet. These forensic analytical tools are stored in the Forensics Media Library built within the DFET project and are triggered for use during the training process. Another key part of the process intended for education and training is the in-built metrics for the assessment of the trainee's performance. These metrics are related to the following:

The time necessary to find the required evidence (which is limited in accordance with some difficulty level that is specified in advance);
The investigation method used;
The application of the right parameters/indicators within the applied forensic tool.

The parameters identifying the factual, conceptual, procedural and metacognitive learning outcomes are introduced in the assessment part of the educational tool. Here, we present only the main training process by providing an explanation of the properties of the EduFors tool.

3 The EduFors Tool

3.1 Basic Architecture Description

The tool is designed to generate instances based on known cybercrime scenarios and to present them to the trainee. The required levels of skills and understandings to solve the challenge are accommodated in such a way that it reflects the different educational levels to be employed for the different trainee groups. The EduFors tool consists of two parts: the front end, which communicates (using an API – Application Interface) with the backend, which is responsible for the generation of the instances representing different situations and for the management of the training process. The front end allows the trainees to enrol in the system and to gain access to all the available courses for their level of education. The appointed administrator creates paths for accessing the courses, giving assignments to the trainees and manages the virtual machines generated in different platforms available in the cloud. This part of the system is also responsible for the presentation of the log files, the generation of the images and the injection of standardized templates for each of the crime scenarios that is selected to be examined by the trainee. The tool is also responsible for managing the virtual machines on the remote cloud platforms. Representational State Transfer (REST) access is used (REST over the HTTP protocol) for communications with the remote terminal used by the trainee. The data are exchanged in the JSON format.

The registration of the trainee is enabled by direct self-registration or via a social network account (e.g., Facebook). Adding a new course to the system is fairly straightforward, as just the title and the description of the course are required to be entered, together with the duration of the course, accompanied by the course material. Once the trainees are registered and the courses saved in the system, the administrator starts with the preparation of the virtual forensic machines. Six combinations of cybercrime scenarios are currently available in the EduFors tool, but there are plans to add more. Every time the administrator creates a new virtual machine for each of the existing scenarios, a different dynamic attack is applied to this machine. Figure 2 shows the list of pre-created virtual machines and the available crime scenarios, stored on the forensic disks, with the crime-attack data that are afterwards embedded in each template presented to the trainee. The dynamic templates for each type of criminal attack and for each trainee are unique because of the different instances and the injected data.

Each of the criminal attacks is presented to the trainee as a standard template, stored on the virtual machine with the respective forensic disk. The templates presented to the trainee differ in terms of the injected data from the templates presented to another trainee and regarding the required level of skills and knowledge that a particular cybercrime case requires to be solved and for the production of evidence.

3.2   Training Scenarios and Assignments

Currently, the EduFors tool generates dynamic forensic templates for the three most frequent cybercrime scenarios: phishing, SQL-based data leakage and a distributed denial-of-service (DDOS) attack. However, in the next version of the tool other cybercrime scenarios will be added according to the definition in the ISO standard [10]. We present all of them briefly, as follows.

Phishing. In this scenario, the client Adam discovers that his bank account has been compromised using a phishing method. The scenario is constructed with the use of two virtual machines (A and C) and a bank server. The attacker has obtained access to the server C by exploiting weak password protection, as he/she has created a fake website as an imitation of the client bank's server. By sending forged emails to Adam, and inviting him to access his bank, the attacker tricks him into believing that he is actually accessing his trusted bank website. That causes the client A to send personal information to the fake host, residing on the attacker server C, and misleading him into believing that he was exchanging information with the bank (server B). The implementation of the

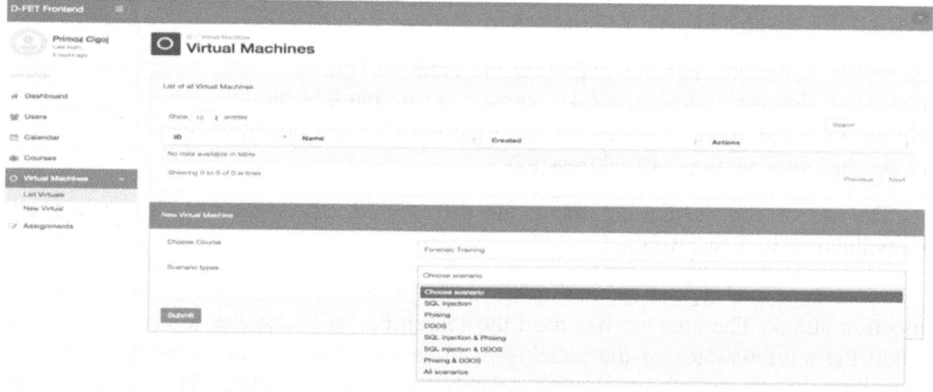

Fig. 2. The EduFors forensic virtual machines

phishing scenario and the data capture for forensic analyses require a website that retrieves and stores the entered credentials, the MySQL database for storing the retrieved credentials and various server log files. The log files contain the data of the random accesses to the phishing site by the victims and by the attacker. The instances and the template data are provided by a script, written in PHP language, that uses two parameters – the test name and the test sequence number, for example, "phishing 1". The script then runs the attack scenario by picking up a random date for the time when the attack occurred. A list of template logs is then preloaded from the template folder, which is then used to generate the victim logs in the Apache OS and for the MySQL log files. This script is executed on a special virtual machine that has access to the VMware platform of the cloud and the data storage. The attacker's template is selected and the placeholders are replaced with randomly selected data. These random data are built up from the IP address, the date and the hour of the accesses. The IP address is unique to the whole log and is not repeated for any other victim logs. The populated template, based on these data, is then stored within the output file for the trainee. Each training day can have a random number of events (between 6 and 24). To make the attacker's footprint slightly harder to find by the trainee, additional data lines are added at the top of the log files (adding data for several days up to 10). The same is applied to the end of the log files (for 1–10 days). The days are generated incrementally and de-incrementally from the remainder of the generated log, so the resulting logs are listed in chronological order. The results are stored in the local MySQL database (the attacker's IP address, the date and the hour of the attack and the type of scenario). A prepared, empty, virtual disk image is copied and mounted as a local file system using the libguestfs tool [11]. The logs are then injected inside the virtual disk image, the virtual machine template is cloned on the VMware server and the modified disk image is uploaded to the data storage. In this way it is possible to enable a new virtual machine to be prepared for inspection of the forensic image. The results, along with the virtual-machine identification, are then returned as an output in the JSON format. The trainee receives a template of Adam's PC and the templates from the compromised server. In this scenario, the assignment given to the trainee consists of the following tasks:

find the IP source address of the attacker,

explain how the attacker has exploited the bank server,
locate the directory where the fake website of the bank is hidden,
explain how the attacker stored the required data for the phishing scenario,
locate the other victims' IP address(es).

The answers to these assignments are then stored, the correctness is checked, and an evaluation is then provided.

Data Leakage and SQL Exploit. In this scenario, a website is the victim of an SQL injection attack. The attacker has used the search bar to access the website's database. When the administrator of the attacked web server comes to the conclusion that the web data are compromised, he immediately contacts the police. The server is then disabled to prevent any further exploitation by the attackers and the logs are brought to the trainee.

The crime scenario for the data leakage and the SQL exploitation are implemented using the same script as for the phishing scenario, but the task generation is based on different log templates and website structures. The websites are modified so that they become vulnerable to SQL injection, which allows the attacker to run a multi-query MySQL statement, including uploading a binary file and saving it directly within a web-accessible folder. This attack is accomplished with an open-source tool known as SQL-Map, which implements the SQL injection method and allows the execution of the remote SQL statements. Several security features of the configured machine for training must be disabled as the most recent OS Ubuntu software versions contain patches that solve the so-far identified security vulnerabilities. We mention some of them here: prevention of writing MySQL data inside the Apache's/var/www/html folder, and removal of the MySQL access to the group www-data, etc. In the Ubuntu OS other security features were also introduced, such as the prevention of the use of the multi-query MySQLi function, which allowed the execution of additional full SQL statements (as opposed to generally used, single-query, MySQLi functions that are not vulnerable to SQL injection attacks).

The file that generates the template data for this type of attack is a PHP script in the form of a web file that allows simpler uploading for larger additional scripts. This scenario uses a publicly accessible PHP shell and a multipurpose script known under the acronym "cyb3r sh3ll". By exploiting these scripts, the attacker can retrieve various types of information from the server database, and each case of access generates a different set of data that is retrieved by the attacker. The script that generates the log files for the trainee uses another type of template. The template matches the specific filenames of the attack scripts and the SQL queries that they execute. As an addition to the MySQL log, the script attaches the SQL injection query that has executed the attack. The assignments for this scenario given to the trainee are as follows:

Decide whether it has come to an SQL injection on the particular identified server;
Identify the IP source address of the attacker;
Find which data were compromised;
Fix the attacked website.

Distributed Denial-Of-Service (DDOS). A DDOS scenario is implemented using the same script as phishing and data leakage, but the log templates presented to the trainee are different. This attack is implemented by simulating a small-scale DDOS attack that is initiated from different machines. Some of them are just normal computer-machine clients, but the others are virtual. The network traffic for the required evidence is captured on the victim's server. The script for this scenario picks a random date to indicate the date when the attack has occurred. A list of template logs is then preloaded from the template folder to the Apache server log files and presented to the trainee. The assignments given for this type of tasks are as follows:

Decide whether it has come to a DDOS attack;
Identify the IP source address of the attacker(s);
Find if a botnet network was involved in the attack;
Assess the damage, taking into account the time for which the server was disabled;

The processes run by the EduFors tool during the laboratory training are presented in Fig. 3.

3.3   The Training Exercise

Each training includes laboratory work constructed from the assignments generated by the EduFors tool. The assignments are presented to the student as a choice of the available scenarios prepared for a particular educational level and the associated laboratory training. The student selects a one-by-one scenario as a result, and finishes the training after all the task assignments have been solved successfully. After the student finishes the assignment tasks, the educator evaluates the used time and the correctness of the solved forensic problem(s) provided by the EduFors tool.

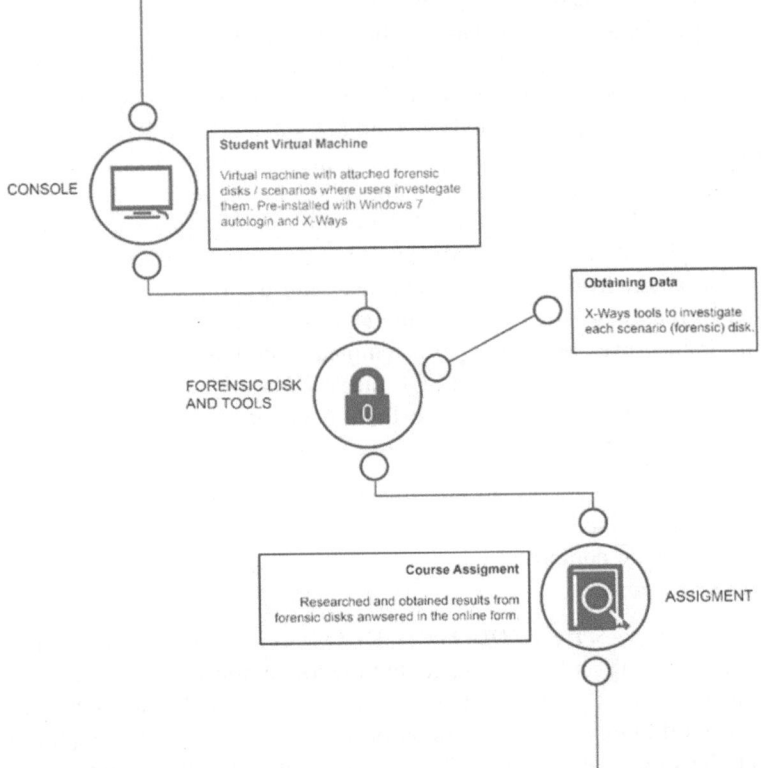

Fig. 3. EduFors process

The tool collects the following data: the time slot between the opening of an assignment and its closing, and the time the student has used to accomplish the task or to answer the questions. If the time spent for solving the tasks is longer than the pre-allocated time for each task, this is acknowledged to the educator and a negative point is entered into the calculated scores for the correct answers. The allocated time per assignment differs and depends on the difficulty level required for the task solving. If 50 % of the answers submitted by the student are correct and the time is not exceeded, then a positive score is given by the tool to this trainee. However, this percentage can be changed by the educator, depending on his/her requirements. To each participant in the training, e.g., trainee, educator and administrator, a different dashboard view of the tool EduFors is provided and this feature allows a visible follow up of the performed tasks and the achieved level of success for each of them.

The EduFors tool was recently launched and used in one of the seminars offered by the MSc program of the International Postgraduate School Jožef Stefan, so exhaustive experience cannot be reported yet. However, the first feedbacks from the educators and the trainees are very positive.

4 Conclusion

Teaching digital forensics is a demanding area of education as it involves intensive, hands-on exercises that require students to follow potentially tedious procedures that demand a long and focused span of attention. Due to these challenges, current forensics courses are often designed for advanced students that are capable of following a variety of demanding disciplines from OS, IP networking and traffic monitoring, file system analysis, basic web applications or protocols. The knowledge of these disciplines is a prerequisite for digital forensic students, so that they are capable of absorbing advanced, abstract concepts used in discovering acts of cybercrime and frauds. The experiments used for training are usually tedious, static and are not frequently applied during the study. In this paper we have proposed an innovative idea to overcome some of the difficulties associated with digital forensics education, based on a successful combination of the visualization technologies and the dynamic generation instances in a real cloud-based computing environment. The current experiences point to the conclusion that this approach will be very effective in the teaching of digital forensics and in other advanced, computer-based fields that involve an understanding of abstract concepts and hands-on practice. Future work includes upgrading the EduFors tool with game elements that will contribute to the attractiveness of EduFors applications and for triggering more attention from the learners and educators. We also plan to work on a further assessment and evaluation for measuring the effectiveness of the presented educational approach.

References

1. Downes, S.E.: Learning 2.0. The eLearn Magazine (2005). http://www.elearnmag.org/subpage.cfm?section=articles&article=29-1. Accessed 12 December 2014
2. Massachusetts Institute of Technology: Open course ware project. http://ocw.mit.edu/index.htm. Accessed 1 December 2014
3. Pollitt, M., Nance, K., Hay, B., Dodge, R.C., Craiger, P., Burke, P., Brubaker, B.: Virtualization and digital forensics: a research and education agenda. J. Digital Forensic Pract. 2(2), 62–73 (2008)
4. Gottschalk, L., Liu, J., Dathan, B., Fitzgerald, S., Stein, M.: Computer forensics programs in higher education: a preliminary study. In: Proceedings of the ACM SIGCSE Bulletin, vol. 37, no. 1, pp. 147–151. ACM Press, St. Louis (2005)

5. Taylor, C., Endicott-Popovsky, B., Phillips, A.: Forensics education: assessment and measures of excellence. In: 2007 Second International Workshop on Systematic Approaches to Digital Forensic Engineering, pp. 155–165. IEEE (2012)
6. Hartel, P., Junger, M., Wieringa, R.: Cyber-crime science = crime science + information security. twente university report. http://www.eprints.eemcs.utwente.nl/18500/. Accessed 1 December 2014
7. D-FET project. http://www.d-fet.eu/project-overview/. Accessed 5 December 2014
8. Laisheng, X., Zhengxia, W.: Cloud computing a new business paradigm for E-learning. In: Proceeding of International Conference on Measuring Technology and Mechatronics Automation, pp. 716–719 (2011)
9. ISEC: Prevention and fight against crime. http://ec.europa.eu/dgs/home-affairs/financing/fundings/security-and-safeguarding-liberties/prevention-of-and-fight-against-crime/index_en.htm. Accessed 18 Dec 2014
10. ISO, 2012. ISO 27037:2012: Information technology — security techniques — guidelines for identification, collection, acquisition, and preservation of digital evidence. Accessed 2 March 2015
11. Diagnostics for libguestfs. http://libguestfs.org/libguestfs-test-tool.1.html. Accessed 5 December 2014

On Experience of Using Distance Learning Technologies for Teaching Cryptology

Sergey Zapechnikov, Natalia Miloslavskaya[✉],
and Vladimir Budzko

The National Research Nuclear University MEPhI
(Moscow Engineering Physics Institute), 31 Kashirskoye Shosse, Moscow, Russia
{SVZapechnikov,NGMiloslavskaya}@mephi.ru

Abstract. The necessity of using Distance Learning (DL) for teaching cryptology is analyzed. The modern features of applying different DL approaches to solve this task are extracted. The NRNU MEPhI's experience in creating mass-oriented DL project called Cryptowiki.net is described; its structure and assignments implemented by the students of cryptologic courses are shown. The related works are presented. Cryptowiki.net's difference from the analogs is stressed out. The main findings of the research are formulated in conclusion.

Keywords: Cryptology · Teaching cryptologic courses · Mass-oriented distance learning technologies

1 Introduction

Distance learning (DL) can be defined as a teachers-students interaction at a distance that reflects all the typical learning process's components (objectives, contents, methods, organizational forms, and learning tools) and is realized by the specific means of the Internet technologies or another tools providing interactivity [1, 2]. Even a new cryptology concept was formed: "Modern cryptography is concerned with the construction of information system that is robust against malicious attempts to make these systems deviate from their prescribed functionality" [3].

The comprehensive DL technologies' (DLT) development is one of the global trends widely supported by almost all universities being at the first places in the world rankings like THE (Times of Education), Quacquarelli Symonds (QS) World University Rankings, Shanghai ranking and others. This trend also affects teaching of different subjects in the field of information security and cryptology in particular. However, the widespread DLT usage for teaching cryptology observed today is due to not only the "spontaneous" world trends, but it is also prepared by a number of objective conditions discussed below.

The subject area of cryptology has significantly expanded over the past two decades. Many new applications and corresponding new scientific and methodological apparatus have appeared. At the same time there is a stabilization (or even some decrease) of scientists' and practitioners' interest to the specific sections of classical cryptology or

M. Bishop et al. (Eds.): WISE9, IFIP AICT 453, pp. 111–121, 2015.
DOI: 10.1007/978-3-319-18500-2_10

relatively new sections which were developed dynamically up to this moment. Such significant changes are due to, on the one hand, the rapid information technologies (IT) development and the growing needs of society in ensuring IT security, and on the other hand, new scientific discoveries in cryptology and related fields of applied mathematics. The universities teaching cryptologic disciplines were faced the problem of adequately addressing the extraordinary changes, taking place in the field of computer science in general and in cryptology in particular, in their curricula and educational practice.

The steady and rapid growth of scientific publications in the field of cryptology is observed around the world in recent years. The publications' statistics in the electronic preprint archive of the International Association for Cryptologic Research (IACR) for 1996–2014 (Fig. 1) is a vivid evidence of this fact [4].

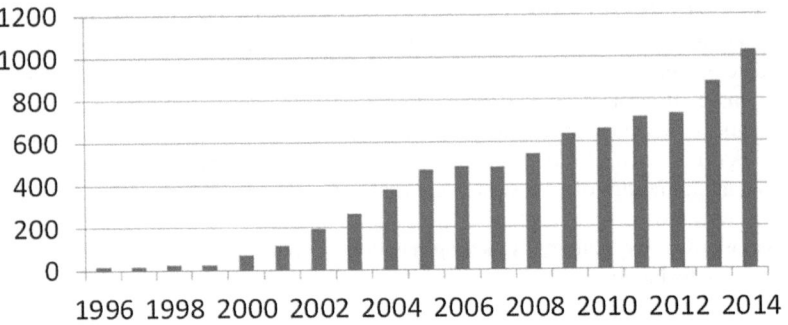

Fig. 1. Publications' statistics in the IACR's electronic preprint archive

In addition the fact that the scientific and technical information search capabilities were fundamentally changed with the advent of the Internet search services like Google, Yahoo!, Yandex, etc., Electronic encyclopedias such as Wikipedia, the archives of electronic publications and preprints (for example, CiteSeer, IEEExplore, eprint.iacr.org et al.) cannot be ignored. As our practice shows these services are actively used by the students and teachers to find a proper term, article, book, algorithm, protocol, method or application description, etc.

A teacher's role is fundamentally changing in the context of this "information explosion". In the past he/she was almost the only affordable student's authoritative source of knowledge. Now he/she turns in some sense into a certain filter that should save the students from the huge flow of superfluous, insignificant or frankly false information and give them only high-quality and systematically organized knowledge. In these circumstances the teacher's task is to organize an educational process in such a way that will maximize the effectiveness of learning and acquisition of the necessary competencies (knowledge, skills and abilities) by the students.

The remainder of the paper is organized as follows. Section 2 includes an overview of related works. Different DLT applications are analyzed in Sect. 3. Section 4 introduces the NRNU MEPhI's experience in applying the mass-oriented DLT in the form of the Cryptowiki.net site. The main findings of the project are formulated in conclusion.

2   Related Works

Of course our idea to create a specialized DL site in not novel. The sharply increasing interest to DL has led to the emergence of a number of DL courses on cryptology in English (with rare exceptions) at present. The courses offered by the MOOC systems (from *Massive Open Online Courses*) should be noted among them first of all.

The "Cryptography I" course is already available and the "Cryptography II" course is going to start from June 2015 in the Coursera system; both courses are authored by the famous Stanford University's Professor Dan Boneh [5].

The Udacity portal offers the "Applied Cryptography" online course conducted by the University of Virginia's Professor Dave Evans [6].

Three courses ("Cryptography and Cryptanalysis", "Advanced Topics in Cryptography", and "Selected Topics in Cryptography") are available at the online educational portal of the Massachusetts Institute of Technology (MIT) [7].

In addition to the online courses a number of carefully designed offline courses on cryptography well suited for self-training can be found on the Internet (not only in the form of lectures' video records and forums that allow to meet with a teacher, but also as notes, lectures, tutorials, home works and their solutions, sample exam assignments, etc.). For example, the courses such as "Modern Cryptography" and "Advanced Cryptography" by Professor Mihir Bellare and Professor Phillip Rogaway from the University of California at San Diego [8], "Cryptographic Protocols" by Ueli Maurer from the ETH Zurich University [9], and "Introduction to Cryptography" by Rafael Pass from the Cornell University [10] can be mentioned here.

It is often recommended for the students to use a wiki as a reference tool in some online courses. That mainly affects the sections not included in the curriculum body (typically the wiki textbooks are additional, not obligatory parts of a taught course) and submitted to their independent study. For example, D.Boneh recommends using the wiki tutorial on the basics of discrete mathematics and discrete probability posted on the popular Wikibooks site as a complement to the above courses [11]. The wiki book on cryptography can be found at the same site [12], but it still looks unfinished.

The given brief analysis shows the necessity of developing a consolidating bilingual (English-Russian) Internet resource in the form of web site containing systematized information on cryptology.

3   Distance Learning Technologies' Application Scenarios

Since cryptology itself is a part of computer science for a long time, the IT role in teaching cryptologic disciplines is dual in modern conditions: they are both a study subject and the tools for organizing an educational process. DLT have the leading role among these tools [13].

At present DLT are quite clearly divided into two sectors: mass-oriented "stream" (large-scale) learning and individual-oriented "chamber" learning.

The first type of technologies is called MOOC. There are the completely-ready-to-use educational products including both learning tools and information resources available online to a potentially unlimited number of trainees via the web interface. In addition to the traditional courses the MOOC's users may have an access to the new educational resources (videos, interactive tasks' sets and assignments in programming, as well as users' forums), enabling to establish an original community of students, professors and teachers being involved in the educational process [14].

The main MOOC idea is realized most completely in the DL Networks (DLN) available via portals, accumulating extensive themed sets of courses in various subject areas. The characteristics of the most-known and popular DLN are shown in Table 1.

Table 1. Most-known DLN on the Internet

DLN name	Internet address	Founders	Number of available courses			Price; Certificate issuance
			2012	2013	2014	
Coursera	coursera.org	Universities: Stanford, Princeton, Berkley, Ohio, Pittsburg, Illinois, Toronto, Georgia, Virginia	207	553	1127	Free; certificates are issued at the end of some courses
edX	edx.org	Universities: Harvard, Massachusetts, Berkley, since 2013 – Texas	9	110	429	Resources – free; certificates are now free; will be paid in future
UM Global Academy	umga.miami.edu	University of Miami	Middle school (MS) – 39, High school (HS) – 91	MS – 39, HS – 73	MS – 39, HS – 74	Access to all resources and courses – $70 registration fee
Udacity	udacity.com	Private company	18	33	60	Free
MIT Open Coursware	ocw.mit.edu	Massachusetts Institute of Technology	2100	2150	2150	Resources – free; certificates are not issued

The high quality of all DLN educational resources and significant increase in the number of available courses should be marked. The number of trainees for the most successful courses is measured by tens and hundreds of thousands worldwide. For example, the "Artificial Intelligence" course from the Coursera network is a leader with more than 180,000 people signed up all over the world at the same time. Such courses being once "put on a stream" are as a rule repeated periodically in the future.

Focusing on such a large audience determines the MOOC's characteristics:

- lack of the students' online feedback to a teacher during the sessions (as the main educational form is a video lecture);
- home works' and long-term projects' check implementation: knowledge progress testing is carried out either by choosing a correct answer from the given set and filling out some online form with automatic check of formats and value meanings entered, or by mutual check and review performed by the students themselves.

In almost all DLN listed in Table 1 the courses in cryptology are presented, for example: "Cryptography I" and "Cryptography II" (D. Boneh) in the Coursera network, "Applied Cryptography" (D. Evans), "Computer Security" conducted by the Stanford University together with the University of California, Berkley (USA) in the same network and several courses on network security and cryptography (both more general and more specialized) in the MIT Open Courseware network (USA).

According to the authors' opinion the obvious advantages of the DLN courses are their high quality and minimum price. That allows to recommend them for self-training to the universities' teaching staff as well as to the students studying on different degrees. The DLN courses being taken together cover all the stages of education – from under-graduate to postgraduate, from Bachelors to Masters and PhD.

However the technologies oriented on massive training do not limited to DLN. They are based on the web technologies as it has been already mentioned. Therefore the creation of multifunctional web sites supporting the educational process and implementing various forms of teachers-students interaction can also benefit.

Technologies of the second type (oriented on individual learning) are essentially different types of videoconferencing with one or more leading (professor/instructor) and a small number of participants actively involved in the process of interaction with the leading. They have a special name – webinars, resulting from compound of the words "web" and "seminar", i.e. a seminar conducted using the web technologies (another names are online seminars, web conferences). All the webinar's participants should either install the special software on their computers or use the special web services provided by several service providers on the Internet. The best-known examples are the services such as Cisco WebEx, Citrix Online, Microsoft Office Live Meeting, HP video conferencing & HP Halo telepresence solutions. However, the number of solutions is increasing every day.

As practice shows the webinars are well suited for the lectures and seminars on different subjects, in particular, a wide range of IT-related disciplines. Currently, some Russian training centers and universities (like the NRNU MEPhI since 2012) implement a few training courses in "Information Security" in the form of webinars.

We would like to point out another model of IT application, having great potential for teaching the cryptologic disciplines. It is no secret that the universities have a very strong and old tradition of "theorizing" (sometimes too redundant) many subjects being taught at the higher school. The reason is the pronounced orientation toward the mass training of scientific and pedagogical personnel required in the past. However, a signif-icant increase in demand for developing the students' practical skills and abilities in using the latest hardware and software and acquisition of practical experience in chosen speciality is observed due to the changes in economic and social life taking place over the past two decades all over the world. The laboratory facilities of many universities and their funding level are not always fully prepared to meet these requirements. At the same time open source software usage is significantly expanding all over the world. In most cases the license agreements for such software allow either its completely free usage for any purpose or at least free usage for non-commercial and educational projects. Free software emerging in the Internet and having a lot of potential applications in cryptology training and its mastering (in particular the development of new labs and practical assignments) can significantly enhance the practical focus of the updated cryptologic courses. The specific examples of such open source software are the libraries of cryptographic algorithms Crypto++, PyCrypto, the prototyping tool for cryptographic constructions Charm, the theoretical and numerical library NZmath and many others.

4   Experience of Mass-Oriented Distance Learning Technologies' Application

The creation of the Cryptowiki.net site supporting educational process for the cryptologic disciplines at the "Information Security of the Banking Systems" Department of the NRNU MEPI is an example of the first type of DLT application.

The site available at http://cryptowiki.net is used as a reference and information resource for professionals in the field of cryptography and for all kinds of students' home and independent works in their study of the "Cryptographic Protocols and Standards"

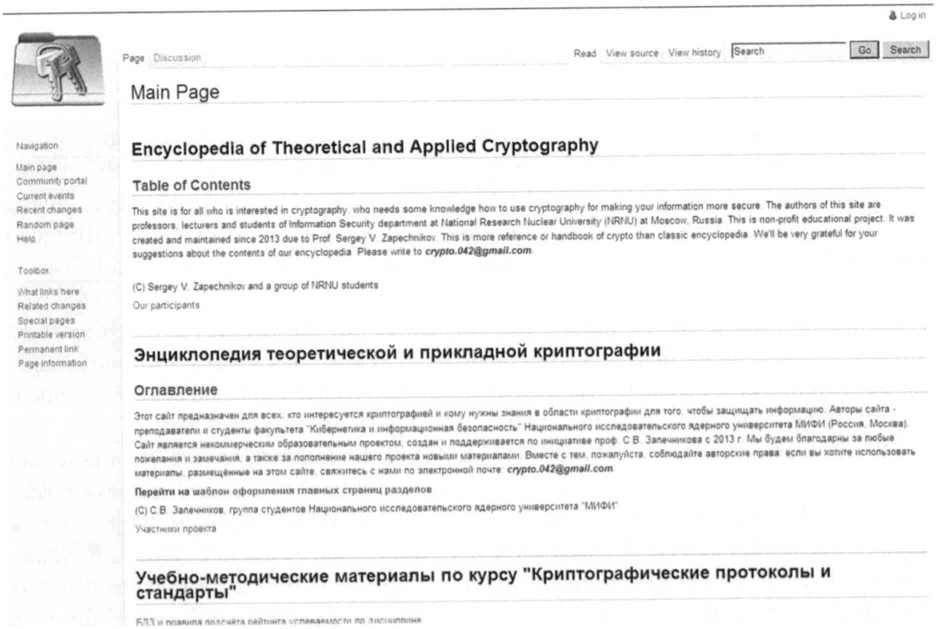

Fig. 2. Cryptowiki.net home page

and "Cryptography in Banking" courses. The site contains various materials for the students' work, rules description for the progress testing rating system and records of webinars previously conducted by the courses' author (Professor S. Zapechnikov).

The site operates under OS Windows on the commercially available hosting with a free content management system (engine) MediaWiki, version BitNami.

cryptowiki.net interface is similar to the Wikipedia interface, well known to the absolute majority of users (Fig. 2).

The central place on the site is allocated to the reference and information system called the "Encyclopedia of Theoretical and Applied Cryptography" (further Encyclopedia). This is a comprehensive information resource created by the joint efforts of the teachers and students, which includes all content types available for posting: text, graphics, video, demo programs, mathematical expressions, program fragments' listings and others.

The Encyclopedia consists of 56 substantive sections, each of which is dedicated to one of the major areas of modern cryptography and is available both in English and Russian languages. The Encyclopedia currently includes the following sections.

Part I "Foundations of Cryptography (Cryptographic Primitives)" consists of 25 sections covering all the main sections of the mathematical apparatus used in modern cryptography and the main types of cryptographic constructions such as block and stream ciphers, hash functions, open encryption schemes, digital signature scheme, as well as numerous supporting questions.

Part II "Applications of Cryptography (Cryptographic Protocols)" includes 31 chapters and is devoted to the cryptographic protocols' design and analysis. It gives knowledge on Zero-knowledge proofs, identification protocols, key distribution protocols, Secret sharing schemes, Threshold cryptography, Byzantine agreement protocol, Fair exchange, Protocols for secure communication channels, Protocols for secure databases retrieval, Protocols for secure cloud computing and secure cloud storage, Protocols for mobile security, Secure multi-party computations and many other cryptographic applications.

Detailed Encyclopedia's content is presented in Table 2.

The site's sections essentially differ from the majority of online information resources by their content's volume and depth. It should be noted that the site is a joint textbook on theoretical and applied cryptography, co-written by students and teachers. However, its content is more focused at people experiencing practical needs in cryptography usage at their workplace, rather than cryptographers–theorists. Most sections do not present the formulations and rigorous proofs of theorems and propositions, but each section contains extensive information on the best-known methods and algorithms for solving the corresponding cryptographic tasks, especially their implementation, allowing to ensure high performance, to avoid vulnerabilities and to achieve ease of use of cryptographic mechanisms by their customers.

In comparison with the traditional textbooks the site's content can be replenished quicker, but of course it is not edited so carefully as for "paper" publishing.

There are some sections, which cannot be found in traditional textbooks. For example, the "Overview of cryptographic primitives: Roadmap for cryptographers" section provides a roadmap of cryptography primitives usage for security tasks' decision. That

Table 2. Cryptowiki Encyclopedia's content

Part I "Foundations of Cryptography (Cryptographic Primitives)"	Part II "Applications of Cryptography (Cryptographic Protocols)"
(1) Brief overview of cryptography;	(1) The basics of cryptographic protocol construction and analysis;
(2) Mathematical background;	(2) Zero-knowledge proofs;
(3) Classical cryptography: experience and lessons;	(3) The framework for identification protocols;
(4) Perfectly-secret ciphers and Shannon's theory;	(4) The framework for key distribution protocols;
(5) Cryptographic generators. Stream ciphers and their cryptanalysis;	(5) Secret sharing schemes. Threshold cryptography;
(6) Block ciphers and their cryptanalysis;	(6) Byzantine generals' problem. Byzantine agreement protocol. Security of distributed computing;
(7) Symmetric encryption schemes;	(7) Fair exchange;
(8) Symmetric message authentication schemes based on block ciphers;	(8) Privacy-preserving collaborative optimization;
(9) Cryptographic hash functions;	(9) Hardware and embedded cryptography;
(10) Symmetric message authentication schemes based on cryptographic hash functions;	(10) Cryptographic libraries for software developers;
(11) Symmetric authenticated encryption schemes;	(11) Vulnerabilities and security of software cryptography;
(12) Symmetric encryption schemes with special features or additional functionality;	(12) Remote authentication protocols and "single sign-on" mechanisms;
(13) Symmetric key management;	(13) Protocols for secure communication channels;
(14) More mathematical background for asymmetric cryptography;	(14) Wireless networks security;
(15) Computationally hard problems used in asymmetric cryptography;	(15) Secure e-mail;
(16) Algorithms used in asymmetric cryptosystems;	(16) Secure instant messaging;
(17) Public key exchange;	(17) Anonymity networks;
(18) Asymmetric encryption schemes;	(18) Protocols for secure databases retrieval;
(19) Digital signature schemes;	(19) Protocols for secure cloud computing and secure cloud storage;
(20) Pairing-based asymmetric cryptosystems;	(20) Protocols for mobile security;
(21) Digital signatures with special features or additional functionality;	(21) RFID security;
(22) Asymmetric key management;	(22) Grid security;
(23) Physically unclonable functions;	(23) Peering networks security;
(24) Standardization of cryptographic methods;	(24) Secure payment systems;
(25) Overview of cryptographic primitives: Roadmap for cryptographers.	(25) Secure broadcasting. Digital content copyright protection;
	(26) Secure multi-party computations;
	(27) Steganography;
	(28) Quantum cryptography;
	(29) Post-quantum cryptography;
	(30) Beyond the post-quantum cryptography;
	(31) Unsolved crypto problems and the future of computer security.

allows the readers to easily navigate the variety of available cryptographic constructions, to choose the most suitable among them for solving their problems and to correctly use it in building their own cryptographic protocol.

Completing assignments, their mutual reviewing by the students and commenting by the teachers on the site create an open and transparent environment for all parts of the educational process, and promote the publicity of students' work results and their objective assessment by the teachers.

An assignment given to the students using the site in the educational process consists of three parts:

1. *content creation for the selected site's section in Russian.* To complete this part of the work it is necessary to create a working team of 2 students (it is allowed to do the work of the whole team alone if a student wants that). The accomplished work is evaluated by the teachers using the 50-points' scale, and the resulting points are distributed among the members of the working team according to their real contribution to the work performed (but not more than 25 points for each member of the working team);

2. *content creation for the selected site's section in English.* The previously formed working teams are kept to perform this work. The site's section content in English should be adequate to the corresponding section in Russian. The slight reductions are allowed in the event of difficulty of the text interpreting in English. The accomplished work is evaluated by the teachers using the same 50-points' scale, and the resulting points are distributed among the members of the working team according to their real contribution to the work performed (but not more than 25 points for each member of the working team). If very many questions to the work performed appear, the team can be called for the oral defense of their work results;

3. *software demo creation demonstrating in practice the execution of one of the cryptographic protocols (algorithms) described in this site's section (or one of the sections created in previous years).* The protocol initial data input (for example long-term and (or) one-time keys, parameters, identifiers, etc.) from files or keyboard and program output to the screen and file should be provided in the program. All arithmetic and logical operations performed by the protocol's parties should be implemented. It is enough to make the program run on one computer and to execute sequentially data input for each of the protocol's parties. Similarly to the output data. Default data input should be provided in case of users' refusal of entering their data. The choice of programming tools and libraries is not limited. The user interface can be arbitrary, but it should be clear to a program's user (for example, the protocol implementation can be presented as a table, similar to those discussed during the lectures). It is desirable, but not required, that the interface will be graphical rather than textual. The program should be run under OS Windows. The program's source code and executables will be available on the corresponding pages of Cryptowiki.net after work will be finalized.

In addition to the Encyclopedia the traditional functionality for educational and methodical sites is implemented on the site: there are a lot of information materials, bulletin board, additional materials for lectures, etc.

5   Conclusion

Summarizing the discussion on applying DLT to teaching cryptology, we would like to note the following.

1. The existing DLT's analysis and the authors' personal experience of their application in teaching cryptology testify that DLT can significantly upgrade all kinds of training – lectures, seminars, and laboratory works. The main positive effect in this case is an increase of educational process's effectiveness, as well as the convenience of teachers-students interaction when performing the home works, course projects, organizational issues and mastering of elective discipline sections.
2. Two pronounced current trends of DLT development are DLN (as well as the related multifunctional web resources that address more narrow audience) and webinars. DLN is the most striking manifestation of emerging global educational space and global competition of the world's leading universities in the educational field. A webinar is the most effective form of classes' organization for the small groups of students. DLT combining both approaches are equally applicable in cryptology training.
3. Our gained experience in applying DLT in teaching cryptology can be extended to the other specialized disciplines taught to the students and trainees of short-term training and long-term professional retraining courses in the "Information Security" direction as well as to supervising the students' educational and scientific research, practical and final qualifying works.
4. The main difference between our CryptoWiki project and its analogs is that it organically complements the lectures and practical works in the cryptologic disciplines, supporting the interactive forms of students' teaching. They feel themselves involved in the process of creating a large-scale Encyclopedia, launched by their predecessors – the students of previous graduation years and planned to continue in the coming years. After graduating from the NRNU MEPhI the former students continue to access the Encyclopedia, in developing which they have contributed, to recommend it to their colleagues and thus spread the cryptologic knowledge.

The project's success is confirmed by the facts that more than 17,000 users have visited the site during the first year of its operation and totally more than 28,000 since 2013.

References

1. Allen, M.W.: Michael Allen's Guide to E-Learning: Building Interactive, Fun, and Effective Learning Programs for Any Company. 2003. 360 p. ISBN: 978-0-471-20302-5
2. Termini i opredelenija distanchionnogo obuchenija. Laboratorija distanchionnogo obuchenija Rossiyskoy Academii Nauk (2015). http://distant.ioso.ru/do/termin.htm. Accessed 24 Feb 2015 (in Russian)
3. Goldreich, O.: Foundations of cryptography – a primer (2015). http://www.wisdom.weizmann.ac.il/~oded/PS/foc-sur04c.ps. Accessed 27 Feb 2015
4. Cryptology ePrint Archive. http://eprint.iacr.org. Accessed 27 Feb 2015

5. Cryptography I. https://www.coursera.org/course/crypto. Accessed 27 Feb 2015
6. Applied Cryptography. https://www.udacity.com/course/cs387. Accessed 27 Feb 2015
7. MIT Open Courseware. http://ocw.mit.edu/courses/find-by-topic. Accessed 27 Feb 2015
8. Courses. https://cseweb.ucsd.edu/~mihir/courses.html. Accessed 27 Feb 2015
9. Information Security & Cryptography (2015). http://www.crypto.ethz.ch/teaching. Accessed 27 Feb 2015
10. Cornell University. Computer Science. Introduction to Cryptography. http://www.cs.cornell.edu/courses/cs4830/2010fa. Accessed 27 Feb 2015
11. High School Mathematics Extensions. http://en.wikibooks.org/wiki/High_School_Mathematics_Extensions/Discrete_Probability. Accessed 27 Feb 2015
12. Cryptography.: http://en.wikibooks.org/wiki/Cryptography. Accessed 27 Feb 2015
13. Anderson, T.: The Theory and Practice of Online Learning, 2nd edn, 484p. AU Press, Athabasca (2008)
14. Waldrop, M.: Massive Open Online Courses, aka MOOCs, Transform Higher Education and Science. Scientific American, April 2013. http://www.scientificamerican.com/article.cfm?id=massive-open-online-courses-transform-higher-education-and-science. Accessed 27 Feb 2015

Syllabus Design

Reflections on the Ethical Content of the IT Honours Program Project Module

Lynette Drevin[(✉)] and Günther Drevin

North-West University (Potchefstroom Campus), Potchefstroom, South Africa
{Lynette.Drevin,Gunther.Drevin}@nwu.ac.za

Abstract. Honours programs in South African universities must include a research project module. There are external pressures from professional bodies and government that influences the nature of the project module. This paper presents a reflection on the process of managing the project module at a South African university taking into account internal and external demands. The focus for this paper is on the ethical content of the projects. Examples of projects are presented after which the ethical awareness of the students is discussed. Not all projects have ethical, legal or social issues, however ethical aspects need to be reflected upon and awareness of these issues is essential during the planning of the project. The awareness that students have on ethical, social and legal issues is investigated in this paper.

Keywords: IT curriculum · Honours project · Research project · Artefact · Information security · Ethics · Social issues · Professional issues · Legal issues · Security awareness

1 Introduction and Background

For many years the honours program in IT, that follows after a three-year bachelor's degree in IT, included coursework as well as a practical project. Currently the honours program in IT at the North-West University consists of coursework (8 semester modules) and a project module. A few years ago government prescription demanded changes to the project module. These changes included a higher number of credits as well as changing the nature of the project to have research oriented content [1]. Currently the number of credits is 32, which implies roughly 320 h of work for a student during an academic year [2].

Recently our institution started a process to get accreditation for the IT program from a professional computer society. In order to align with their requirements another set of demands also surfaced for the project module. One of the main requirements is that the project module must also produce an artefact during the process and not only be a research project. Another demand is the inclusion of legal, social, ethical and professional issues (LSEPI) into the program [3]. With the increased emphasis on ethical issues within organisations as well as government and academic environments this paper explores the topic of ethics and how it is handled in the IT honours project module. The research question for this study of the project module content was: *"How aware are students of ethical and related issues when doing their project?"*

© IFIP International Federation for Information Processing 2015
M. Bishop et al. (Eds.): WISE9, IFIP AICT 453, pp. 125–134, 2015.
DOI: 10.1007/978-3-319-18500-2_11

When reviewing current literature on this topic a leading local university's project module documents were analysed. They indicate a twofold process to obtain permission for a project to progress. A form is completed by the student to get permission to use other students as sources of information (access to students for the purpose of research). The supervisors' details as well as the research proposal are included in this form. This form goes to the director of student affairs. Another form that is needed is the ethical clearance which is submitted to the faculty's ethics committee [4]. Aspects that are covered include:

- Has the student read the university's code where human subjects are involved.
- Is the student familiar with the procedure of collecting data.
- Has enough information been given to the participants.
- Informed consent.
- Permission to conduct the research where student are involved.
- Has anonymity and confidentiality been offered to participants.
- Issues regarding harm to participants or to the university.
- Any other ethical issues.
- Can this project lead to publication and subsequent issues regarding authorship.

Feedback on this process is usually given within a short time in order for the student to make amendments and continue with the project.

From the previous discussion it can be seen that students from this university are guided through the process to reflect on ethical issues and to obtain ethical clearance for their projects.

This paper will focus on the university where the project module has recently been changed and will demonstrate how ethics and related topics such as professionalism and social issues are handled within the project module. The layout of this paper is as follows. The research method will be discussed in Sect. 2. Section 3 presents a discussion of how this project module was managed and executed over the past number of years. Example projects will be discussed in Sect. 4. Thereafter it will be shown how the LSEP issues are incorporated into the module by doing a narrative analysis of each project. The focus in Sect. 5 is on the ethical issues that the students have to identify and reflect on. Section 6 concludes this paper with a summary and possible future work.

2 Research Approach

The main approach to make sense of the project module was to analyse each project in terms of certain factors such as key words used, having a definite Information security content or not, ethical dilemmas identified and reflection of the student and supervisor on the product and process. This paper, however, only focuses on the ethical content to align with the aims and scope of WISE.

The main source of data was the project documentation of the students, e.g. project proposals and projects reports. The proposals and reports were qualitative in nature. Therefore an approach of analysis of data was required to explore the content of the relevant parts, presenting the findings and interpreting it in a way that makes sense of the results. An in depth analysis of what was said and communicated by the students was necessary; therefore narrative analysis was the appropriate approach. Narrative analysis refers to a wide variety of approaches within many disciplines and sub disciplines where interviews and qualitative data are concerned. According to Wood and Kroger [5] the aim is to get a deeper understanding of the phenomenon under investigation. However, there is more than one way of doing this. Each project has its own questions and aims and therefore the researcher has multiple ways to do narrative analysis and interpretation [6]. In this context the reports of the students are the vessels in which content is held [7]. Different topics were examined, retrieved and categorized in order to get a deeper understanding of the ethical issues involved in these honours projects. The yes/no answers in the questionnaires were counted and are shown and discussed in Sect. 5. The students were required to elaborate on these answers and these qualitative data in the reports were analysed using a narrative approach. Short interviews with the lecturers who acted as project supervisors were also conducted and their input to the students on ethical issues will also be presented in Sect. 5 along with the students' reflections on these matters.

The following section presents the management of the project module including some of the internal and external requirements.

3 Project Module Management

The number of students in the IT honours program is between 30 and 40. Around 9 lecturers have to supervise these projects. Normally the lecturers propose project topics, however sometimes students also suggest topics that have to be in line with the necessary requirements. Previously the honours projects that were done by students differed in content and nature. Some students developed a practical system while other projects had a bigger research component. Since 2011 the government prescription that the project must be a research project changed the way in which students and lecturers approached the project [8]. Until 2013 the project module was not fixed in nature and it was difficult to get uniformity with the evaluation of the projects.

In 2014 the nature of the project was changed yet again due to the prescription of being a research project as well as producing an artefact [3]. The process of managing and supervising the project can be summarized as follows [2, 8]:

- The students are given a project module study-guide in which the aim and significance of the project is presented. The manner in which the project is managed is also described, the role of the project supervisors is discussed and teaching, learning strategies and assessment issues are presented. There are guidelines as well as marking schemes for each component of the project.
- The students are also referred to the guidelines of the university regarding postgraduate studies, writing reports and referencing.
- The aim of this module is highlighted to the students as [8]:
  - To enable students to do research, collect and analyse data and write a well-structured report and article of the results, as well as to communicate the research results during a presentation.

- To enable students to apply knowledge of various other modules in the development of an artefact and associated documentation.
- The time duration of the project is from February to October.
- Project assignments: Students are given a choice of topics proposed by the lecturers.
- The role of the lecturer is to supervise the process and give guidance. Weekly consultations are normally held.
- An electronic platform is used for the dissemination of information and documents as well as for the submission of completed components of the project.
- Some of the lecturers also inform students of various aspects of the module e.g. research methods, system development strategies, writing of articles, etc. There is also a project coordinator that oversees these topics.
- Some projects can be done in small groups but each student must individually submit a final report.
- Assessment is done on five components:
  - Project proposal and planning
  - Literature study
  - Artefact, poster and documentation
  - Full report and article
  - Presentation.

  For each of these components, dates for completion are given at the beginning of the year. Guidelines and marking sheets are available for each of the components. Both the supervisor as well as a moderator assesses each component of the project. All the lecturers assess the presentations. The students also do a peer-assessment of their fellow students' presentations.
- The aspect of ethical, social and legal issues also gets attention. Students are required to do a literature review on ethical issues. As a starting point they are referred to relevant chapters in research methods textbooks. They also have to complete a questionnaire on the relevance of ethical, social and legal issues regarding their own project. In these questionnaires the students have to indicate how they will address these issues in their projects. The questionnaires are included in the project proposal as well as the final report.

  Many textbooks specifically aimed at postgraduate students in IT inform students about ethics in the research process [6, 9]. Olivier [9] for instance discusses examples of unethical situations in the research milieu and in so doing provides the students with insight of what to be cautious about. The practice of having an ethics committee or review board to evaluate research proposals and ethical clearances is also explained. Another textbook prescribed to the honours projects is Oates [6]. Issues that are highlighted in [6] are:
  - The rights of participants in a study: e.g. right to withdraw, right to anonymity.
  - The law and research: e.g. data protection, legal liability when software is developed.
  - Responsibilities of the researcher: e.g. behave with integrity.

    LSEP aspects are also discussed throughout the students' curriculum at different year levels in modules such as programming, system analysis and design, databases, new developments etc. Definitions or broad descriptions of ethics are discussed. An example of a definition of ethics that is used is *"A set of principles that guides decision making based on personal values of what is considered right or wrong"* [10].

- The University has a policy on plagiarism. Students must adhere to these guidelines.
- As part of the final project report the students have to reflect on what they have learnt while completing this project.

As can be seen in the above list ample help was provided to the students regarding time and process management. Regarding ethical issues an effort was made to inform students about ethical and related issues though lectures, references and examples.

The following section describes a few of the projects that were completed during the previous year(s) indicating the variety of project topics.

4 Project Examples

Students can choose from a range of topics for possible projects offered to them at the beginning of the year. These proposals come from the lecturers that have to take on honours projects. These topics originate from their own fields of interest or expertise or research areas. The students select 5 topics in order of their preferences. A committee allocates a topic to each student in such a manner as to assign them, as far as possible, one of their top 3 choices in order for them to be positive towards their topic from the start of their project.

Examples of project topics, with aims or descriptions as well as an indication of possible ethical issues, are [8]:

1. Generating secure passwords through the use of a password generator:
   "The goal of this project is to create a password generator that will help users to protect their data and files from unauthorized access and theft, as well as creating a secure "password vault" that will be used to store the generated passwords so that the users do not need to remember all of them. In order to achieve this, the following objectives must be met:
   - Investigate existing methods for safe storage of passwords.
   - Conduct a survey to access individuals' awareness on password management.
   - Develop an application for individuals to securely store their passwords."
   Analysis: Yes - noticeable ethical issues.
2. Automated Computer Trading System Using Price Action To Predict Currency Movements.
   Analysis: Perhaps – not so obvious to detect ethical issues.
3. Investigation of privacy concerns regarding mobile positioning data:
   "The aim of this project is to investigate privacy concerns of mobile positioning technology. In order to accomplish this, the following objectives need to be reached:
   - Assessment of the privacy issues of mobile positioning technology.
   - Evaluation of privacy awareness of mobile users.

- Develop an application to monitor access to the mobile user's location, in order to improve user's awareness and understanding of their mobile applications usage of their location data.
- Evaluate the usefulness of the application."
Analysis: Yes - noticeable ethical issues.
4. How the programs of the NSA are harming the integrity of the Internet:
Aims:
  - "To critically evaluate the activities of the NSA and how they harm the integrity of the Internet.
  - To inform the public about mass surveillance and what they can do to stop it and how they can protect themselves from it.
  - To identify and critically evaluate the ethical implications of mass surveillance by referring to surveillance and abuse of powers in other countries where mass surveillance is done."
Analysis: Yes - noticeable ethical issues.
5. The development of an android mobile electronic banking application for elderly people:
"The aim of this project is to do thorough research regarding the specific needs of elderly people, and to develop a mobile banking application that will satisfy this target group's needs, if they want to make use of electronic banking services.
Analysis: Yes - noticeable ethical issues.
6. Social engineering: Why the social engineer succeeds?
"Social engineering will be studied as an attack on individuals and organizations to get sensitive or private information. The aim is to analyse and inspect different aspects of a social engineering attack and finally summarize how these different elements contribute to the success of social engineering attacks."
Analysis: Yes - noticeable ethical issues.
7. A group project on game development. Each member in the group did research on a specific aspect of the gaming industry, for example, graphics and software development methodologies. Furthermore, a game was designed and developed by the group as a whole.
Analysis: No – not so obvious to detect ethical issues.

These examples indicate the variety of topics and different fields of interest of supervisors and students. Some project topics have obvious ethical issues while with others such issues only become apparent at later stages.

The next section presents the analysis of the contents of the projects regarding the ethical questionnaire that the students have to complete as part of their project planning as well as their own reflections of these issues.

5 Analysis and Discussion of Ethical Content

Each student has to complete a questionnaire on ethical issues pertaining to their project topic. This questionnaire was developed from example documents, guidelines from the university and prescriptions from external bodies. 33 project reports were used

Table 1. Responses of students to ethical questionnaire

Question	Yes	No	N.A.	No answer
1. Did you read the sections on ethics?	31	0	0	2
2. Do you use people as a source of data?	14	17	0	2
3. Do you need permission.e.g. equipment?	11	20	0	2
4. Assured confidentaiality for participants?	19	6	6	2
5. Damage/harm to environment/participants?	4	26	1	2
6. Risk to institution?	2	28	0	3
7. Any other ethical issues?	7	23	0	3

as data and analysed. The questions that were asked in the questionnaire, which they had to reflect upon and get more information on, are listed in Table 1.

1. In general all the students indicated that they read the sections on ethics in research in the prescribed documents and textbooks. Two students did not include their ethics questionnaire in their proposal or report. (Thus they did not adhere to the mark sheet and requirements of the layout of the required documents). One of these students, however, did include a discussion of the ethical issues of his project in his ethical literature study.
2. 42 % of students conducted a survey or used people as a source of data. It was then compulsory to assure the respondents that their data will be used in a confidential way and their privacy will be protected. This was done as can be seen in the fourth question where 19 of the 33 students gave the assurance of confidentiality to their respondents.
3. 11 Students needed special equipment and had to make arrangements for equipment such as Raspberry Pi boards, Apple computers, Lego Mindstorm sets, etc. They had to make sure that they used the equipment in an orderly and secure manner.
4. Further investigation was done into the apparent discrepancy between questions 2 and 4. Although 42 % said people are used as data sources and 57.6 % indicated confidentiality to data, 18.2 % indicated that they did not have to assure confidentially and 18.2 % said the question is not applicable. Strictly speaking, these 17 students that said no in question 2 should also have said no in question 4. It seems that there can be confusion of what is applicable or not when people are used as a source of data. This needs to be clarified to students in future.
5. 78.8 % of students indicated that no harm could be done to people or the environment when conducting the project. The 4 students that answered yes to this question had to take due care not to let this principle slip. This question relates directly to the content of the code of ethics/conduct of the ACM and BCS [11, 12].
6. 28 students indicated that there would not be any harm to the university while conducting their research project. The 2 yes answers concerned the use of university equipment and software licensing.
7. 21 % of student answered yes when asked if there are any other ethical issues regarding their project. These include aspects such as privacy issues in location based applications, moral and psychological implications when developing games,

face recognition in home automation applications, commercialization of artefacts e.g. intellectual property rights, etc. They had to discuss this with their supervisors and write a section in their report on how this will be handled. Almost 70 % of students did not have any such issues or could not think of any.

Figure 1 presents the seven questions and the responses of the students in a bar graph. It can be seen that the last 3 questions have the most "NO" answers. This may indicate that the ethical concerns relating to people, the environment and the university is minimal. It is not zero, therefore, these issues must definitely be reflected upon and ethical awareness of students is thus necessary.

The students had to expand on the ethical and legal issues that applied to their projects. The following indicates some of these reflections:

- Quite a few mobile applications were developed. With this the aspect of location data had to be taken into account as a possible privacy violation.
- New technology was used. Permission was needed for its use and due care had to be taken while using the hardware.
- The issue of proper licensing of software was also a point to consider. The alternative of using open source software was also suggested.

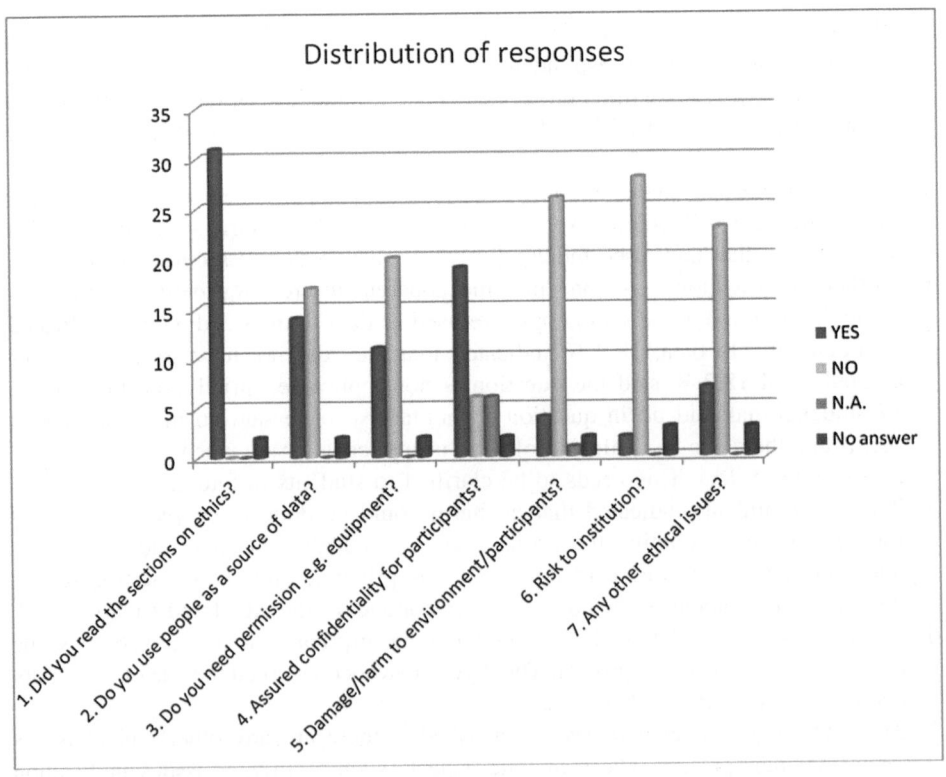

Fig. 1. Distribution of students' responses to ethical questionnaire

- When surveys were done, due care had to be taken to ensure confidentiality of data and identity. Respondents gave informed consent and had the option to withdraw from the study if they wanted to do so.
- In the games project violence was highlighted as a possible moral or ethical issue and age restriction was proposed as a solution. One of the game project students also included a chapter on ethical issues in her final report.
- One project was on the possible damaging effects of mass surveillance. The need of making users aware of these types of actions was highlighted in this project.

The above points demonstrate that students did indeed reflect on social, legal and ethical issues. Table 1 and Fig. 1 indicate in how many of the projects these aspects are present.

After interviewing the supervisors and moderators the following aspects came forth:

- Time management is a huge problem! Although deadlines were given, it was postponed with regularity resulting in a chain effect of accumulation of work.
- Students need to have adequate prerequisite knowledge.
- They need to be enthusiastic about the topic of their project.
- The moderators were mostly satisfied with the process where they assessed different components of different projects.

After the analysis of the interviews with supervisors as well as the students' project documentation a concern that emerged was that the supervisors did not reflect deeply on the ethical aspects and they were easily satisfied that the students did it adequately. Another concern was that not all questions were answered. This should not be allowed.

The university under discussion has a very lengthy application document and process for obtaining ethical clearance for research projects. Therefore an abbreviated document was created for this project module. It is recommended that in future the process for obtaining ethical clearance for honours projects be reconsidered and shortened.

Legal, social, ethical and professional aspects within IT are important and students must be equipped to identify these issues and reflect on how to handle this. The way the ethical questionnaires were filled in and discussed indicates that more guidance is necessary from the supervisors.

The research question that was posed in Sect. 1 was investigated by analysing the narrative content of the students' project documentation. From this analysis it is seen that the students have an adequate sense of ethical and related issues and can approach their work in an ethically responsible manner. However continuous exposure to the importance of LSEP issues remains a challenge in the IT curriculum.

The following section concludes this paper with a summary and some final thoughts.

6   Conclusion

This paper presented a reflection of the handling of the project module for the IT honours program. The manner in which the project module is currently being managed under internal academic demands, external demands from government as well as accreditation requirements was discussed.

Examples of projects were presented (some with specific Information Security content) indicating the increasing importance of the topic of security awareness and expertise of students completing their studies in IT. It is shown how ethical, legal and social issues are included in the project. Lessons learnt from the process are shared in this paper.

Key aspects that came forth from this study include:

– Deeper reflection is needed on ethical aspects by both the students as well as the supervisors. Not all ethical issues are obvious at the beginning of the project;
– Proper completing of the questionnaire;
– Streamlining the ethical clearance process for the project module;
– Continual effort to raise the awareness of these important matters.

For future work reflection of the project process and product is needed and external bodies' input must be evaluated and incorporated into the management of the project module. IT students' awareness, expertise and knowledge regarding ethical issues need to be relevant and processes followed must be adaptable for current and future demands of the industry and related professional IT bodies.

References

1. South Africa: The Higher Education Qualifications Framework, Higher Education Act, 1997 (Act No. 101 of 1997) Government Notice, Department of Higher education, Government gazette, 30353, 3–28, 5 Oct 2007
2. Taylor, E.: Natural Sciences Project: Computer Science and Information Systems. North-West University. (Study-guide ITRI617) (2014)
3. Academy of BCS.: Legal, social, ethical & professional issues (LSEPI). http://academy.bcs. org/content/legal-social-ethical-professional-issues-lsepi(2014). Accessed 21 Jan 2015
4. UCT: Guidelines for Honours Projects. Department of Computer Sciences (2011)
5. Wood, L., Kroger, R.: Doing Discourse Analysis: Methods for Studying Action in Talk and Text. Sage Publications, Thousand Oaks (2000)
6. Clandinin, D.J.: Handbook of Narrative Inquiry. Mapping a Methodology. Sage, Thousand Oaks (2007)
7. Oates, B.: Researching Information Systems and Computing. Sage, London (2006)
8. eFundi.: ITRI 671 P Year 2014: Assignments. http://efundi.nwu.ac.za/portal/site/088f993e-eb52-4964-b315-1a358908cd16/page/acab8dd5-b68b-4191-996b-75f59c4db55. Accessed 18 Jan 2014
9. Olivier, M.: Information technology research. Van Schaik Publishers, Pretoria (2004)
10. Schwalbe, K.: Information technology project management. Course Technology, USA (2014)
11. ACM. Code of Ethics.: Association for Computing Machinery, http://www.acm.org/about/code-of-ethics Accessed 3 Nov 2014
12. BCS.: British Computer Society, Code of conduct for BCS members. http://www.bcs.org/upload/pdf/conduct.pdf (2014)

Professional Competencies Level Assessment for Training of Masters in Information Security

Natalia Miloslavskaya[✉] and Alexander Tolstoy

The National Research Nuclear University MEPhI (Moscow Engineering Physics Institute), 31 Kashirskoye Shosse, Moscow, Russia
{NGMiloslavskaya, AITolstoj}@mephi.ru

Abstract. The peculiarities of assessing the level of professional competency formation in information security (IS) are discussed. The approach described uses the levels of mastering of specific disciplines forming this competency. Professional competencies in the field of information security and their levels are defined. The paper explains how these competencies can be formed. Metrics for the level of mastery of the discipline are introduced. The competencies level assessment model is proposed. The model application to the "Business Continuity and Information Security Maintenance" program for Masters at the NRNU MEPhI is shown. Important notes on using the model are given in conclusion.

Keywords: Masters in information security · Professional competency · Professional competencies level assessment · Professional competencies level assessment model

1 Introduction

A professional in any field of activity must have specific qualifying characteristics. This is also true for the sphere of information security (IS). The modern approach to the determination of qualifying characteristics is based on the definition of professional competencies (further competencies) as a professional's capacity to solve given problems and to perform specific work within his/her sphere of activity [1–3].

Qualifying characteristics for IS specialists can be presented as a set of their competencies in the field of IS (further IS competencies). They are used while implementing organizational personnel policy (including the role identification and assignment, the personnel recruitment and placement) and training (including the definition of requirements that the educational institutions' graduates must meet, and the implementation of an educational process that meets these requirements). Joint efforts of organizations' personnel departments and educational institutions together with the existence of some unified set of competencies will definitely enable coordination of their activities in order to best meet the staffing needs.

A problem of assessing the level of competencies (CL) formed in the implementation of a specific curriculum in the field of IS arises while conducting personnel training in this area. Two approaches are applicable for assessing this level:

© IFIP International Federation for Information Processing 2015
M. Bishop et al. (Eds.): WISE9, IFIP AICT 453, pp. 135–145, 2015.
DOI: 10.1007/978-3-319-18500-2_12

1. Assessment at the training completion (can be done via one single examination on all aspects related to a specific IS competency);
2. Assessment of the levels of mastery of all specific disciplines forming one IS competency.

This paper describes a model that enables us to implement the second approach, which, from our point of view, is more interesting than the first. The remainder of the paper is organized as follows. Professional IS competencies and their levels are defined in Sect. 2. Section 3 explains how these IS competencies can be formed. Section 4 introduces metrics to measure the mastery level of the disciplines. The CL assessment model is proposed in Sect. 5. The model application to the "Business Continuity and Information Security Maintenance" program for Masters at the NRNU MEPhI is shown in Sect. 6. Some important notes on using the model are given in conclusion.

2   Information Security Competencies and Their Levels

Competencies support definitions of job classifications/occupational group profiles, roles and responsibilities, position descriptions, duty statements, etc. [3]. A competency is traditionally defined as a combination of observable and measurable knowledge, abilities and skills (Fig. 1) (as well as individual attributes and work experience) that contribute to enhanced employee performance and ultimately result in organizational success [3, 4].

Knowledge is the cognizance of facts, truths and principles gained from formal training and/or experience.

A skill is a developed proficiency or dexterity in mental operations or physical processes that is often acquired through specialized training; using these skills results in successful performance.

Ability is the power or aptitude to perform physical or mental activities that are often affiliated with a particular profession.

Hence, knowledge, abilities and skills levels are three integral parameters (attributes) of a specific competency, which are necessary to perform a job successfully. In our case this competency is related to the field of IS.

For recruitment it is important not only to formulate all the parameters of a certain competency, but also to determine the necessary levels of these parameters. At present it seems reasonable to use the US Government IS Workforce Development Model defining the following levels of competency [3].

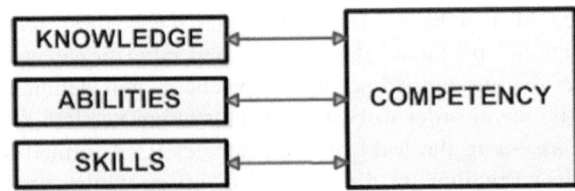

Fig. 1. Three competency's parameters

Level 0 (Not Applicable). The knowledge, abilities and skills levels within the framework of this IS competency are unrelated to the requirements set either by an organization engaged in recruitment for a certain employment or by an institution at a student's training completion.

Level 1 (Entry-Level). The level corresponds to the presence of only basic knowledge in the area of professional activity to which this competency is related (basic under-standing of IS concepts, common knowledge and its application to computer systems architecture) and limited experience (gained in a classroom and/or experimental sce-narios or as a trainee on-the-job) that partially meets the requirements of abilities and skills. A professional has the ability to understand and discuss terminology, concepts and principles, and issues related to this competency. Help or mentoring is needed in performing these skills. The focus is on learning and development of on-the-job experience. When hiring a professional with such CL it is required to provide some mechanism to increase this level. These measures may include training at the work-place under the supervision of experienced staff members or requiring additional training (in the form of retraining courses). In an institution of higher education this level can be raised to the minimum needed to meet the requirements, which charac-terizes the final level of formation of a specific IS competency.

Level 2 (Intermediate). A professional possessing the IS competency of this level demonstrates solid IS knowledge and skills necessary to successfully solve typical professional tasks within the competency and with minimal guidance. He is able to understand and discuss the competency context and implications of changes to pro-cesses, policies and procedures in the professional field. Help or mentoring from an expert may be required from time-to-time (to handle novel or more complex, atypical situations), but the skills can be implemented independently. The focus is on applying and enhancing the levels of IS knowledge and skills. In an educational institution this level characterizes a basic understanding of a specific IS competency.

Level 3 (Advanced). A professional possessing the IS competency of this level has expert understanding, wide knowledge and abilities within that competency. Further, he or she can apply this competency in new or complex situations in related IS areas. He demonstrates expert knowledge of laws, regulations, policies and procedures, and standards in the area of his/her professional activity, including the ability to interpret and to translate subject matter to various audiences and for different applications. This allows him/her to take part in the development of various organizational documents and to focus on broad organizational/professional issues, including participation in senior and executive level discussions regarding this competency. The actions associated with these skills can be performed without assistance and are aimed at solving wide pro-fessional and organizational tasks with a focus on well-organized and accurate work in a team to implement the modern ideas. This professional provides consistent, practical and relevant ideas and perspectives on process or practice improvements, which may easily be implemented. He is a recognized authority within the organization. He is able to coach and mentor others in applying this IS competency by translating complex nuances into easy to understand terms in various business and technology contexts. In an institution this level characterizes an advanced, final level of gaining competency in a specific IS competency.

This paper is focused on solving the problem of assessing the level of IS competency, developed by the students of the higher education institutions.

3 Information Security Competencies Formation

To train IS professionals in an educational institution means to develop the students' IS competencies in a particular area of their professional activity. The existence of such IS competencies when training is complete means the graduate has the ability to perform his job successfully and to solve practical tasks assigned to him by his employer.

Traditional competencies' formation is mastery of a specific number of educational disciplines (further disciplines). In general, they include training courses, various practices (practical works) and completion of a final qualifying work (FQW). One particular institution combined these disciplines to define specific features of an educational program leading to a Bachelor's or Master's degree, or a Specialist diploma, in the IS field [1].

Implementation of a specific programme (for example, for Masters in IS) usually aims to develop some number of students' competencies CJ (Fig. 2). A predetermined number M of disciplines $[D_m]$ $(m = 1, \ldots, M)$ is involved in the formation of each IS competency. A few disciplines directly form a specific competency (e.g. competency C_j). The rest of the disciplines are designed to create the required levels of IS knowledge, abilities and skills, necessary for mastering of disciplines, directly forming all necessary IS competencies. As an example, Fig. 2 shows that N disciplines $[D_{mn}]$ $(n = 1, \ldots, N)$ providing the knowledge, skills and abilities for the discipline D_m.

Thus, the levels of attributes of a specific IS competency are formed directly and indirectly by the levels of IS knowledge, abilities and skills, obtained by mastering of a set of disciplines.

To determine the levels of competency in the various attributes making up IS, we have to measure the levels of mastery of disciplines making up that competency. We must also assess the contribution of each discipline to achieving IS competency.

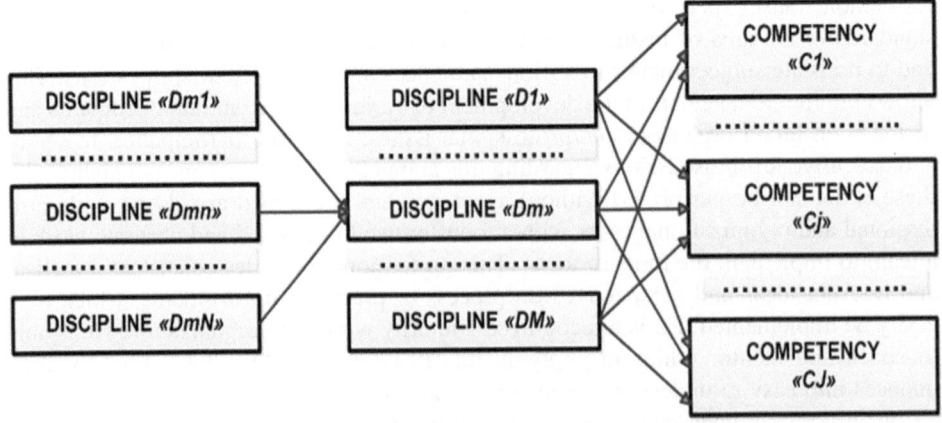

Fig. 2. Diagram of IS competencies' formation

4   Metrics for the Levels of Mastery of the Discipline

Different scales can be used to assess the level of mastery of the discipline (DML). It may be a mark in points from 0 to 100 (Fig. 3a) or 0 to 10 (Fig. 3b), a literal indexing from J to A (Fig. 3c) or a mixed form (Fig. 3d) from 1 ("very bad") to 5 ("excellent"). There are also other assessment scales.

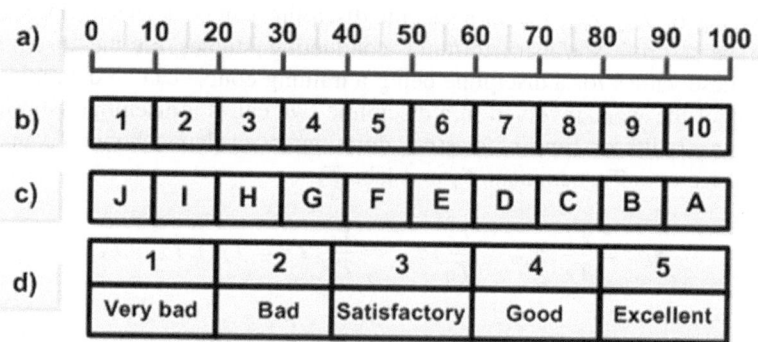

Fig. 3.   Levels of mastery of the IS disciplines

To assess DMLs using CL it is necessary to select a single scale. This paper uses a point scale – from 0 to 100 (Fig. 3a). Converting the measurement of a DML from one scale to another does not pose difficulties in any particular case (Fig. 3 can be used as an example for that purpose).

The assessment of a specific IS DML for D_m designated here as DA_m should integrate the assessments of the level of gained IS knowledge KD_m, the level of formed IS abilities AD_m and the level of acquired IS skills SD_m, developed by mastery of this discipline. Then

$$DA_m = \alpha_{km}KD_m + \alpha_{am}AD_m + \alpha_{sm}SD_m, \tag{1}$$

where $\alpha_{km}, \alpha_{am}, \alpha_{sm}$ are the weights of the contribution of the attributes (knowledge, abilities and skills) into DML. These attributes must satisfy the condition $\alpha_{km} + \alpha_{am} + \alpha_{sm} = 1$.

The levels KD_m, AD_m, SD_m, which the students develop while mastering specific IS disciplines, are defined during the testing of their progress. Students are evaluated in some way, for example by examination. In that case, the control questions for progress testing should be formulated in such a way that these levels can be clearly assessed based on responses to them.

The following features associated with the peculiarities of a specific IS discipline can also be considered. For example, if the discipline is a training course, its curriculum can be implemented using various forms of training: lectures, seminars, and labs. Lectures mainly form the knowledge level, seminars – abilities level and labs – skills level.

If the discipline consists only of the lectures (e.g. a more theoretical discipline studying international law or explaining how to write IS policies), then $\alpha_{km} = 1$, $\alpha_{am} = 0, \alpha_{sm} = 0$.

In case of seminars (e.g. with an assignment to write a specific private IS policy), then $\alpha_{km} \ll \alpha_{am}, \alpha_{km} \leq \alpha_{sm}, \alpha_{am} \geq \alpha_{sm}$.

If nothing but labs (e.g. how to detect network intrusions using IDS predefined for a student or a group of students), then $\alpha_{km} \ll \alpha_{sm}, \alpha_{km} \leq \alpha_{am}, \alpha_{am} \leq \alpha_{sm}$.

In case of practices and FQW, then $\alpha_{km} \leq \alpha_{am}, \alpha_{km} \ll \alpha_{sm}, \alpha_{am} \leq \alpha_{sm}$.

The values of $\alpha_{km}, \alpha_{am}, \alpha_{sm}$ for a specific discipline can be determined by an expert, who can be a professor/instructor/tutor conducting studies on the discipline. For example, these values for a discipline being a training course can be determined based on analysis of the work involved in a discipline (we call it a discipline laboriousness) expressed in credits or time of classes' duration in academic hours T_0 in view of duration of lectures T_k, seminars T_a and labs T_s:

$$\alpha_{km} = \frac{T_k}{T_0}; \alpha_{am} = \frac{T_a}{T_0}; \alpha_{sm} = \frac{T_s}{T_0}; T_0 = T_k + T_a + T_s. \tag{2}$$

5 Information Security Competencies Level Assessment Model

In the introduction we emphasized that we will assess a specific IS competency CA_j and its attributes' values (the levels of IS knowledge KC_j, abilities AC_j and skills SC_j) using the second approach. That approach is based on the characteristics of disciplines forming this competency (DML DA_m, the levels KD_m, AD_m and SD_m).

Let us set the following *assumptions* for the model.

1. Some disciplines D_{mn} are essential for disciplines D_m. These disciplines D_m directly form some IS competency C_j (Fig. 2). Thus, the disciplines D_{mn} indirectly determine the characteristics of the competency C_j. Due to length limits of the paper, we do not consider the characteristics of the underlying disciplines D_{mn}.

2. The results of mastering a specific discipline D_{mn} can be used in the formation of each IS competency C_j connected with this discipline. Therefore, the differentiation of the contribution of a particular discipline into the formation of different competencies is not taken into account.

3. We weight the contributions of a discipline D_m to the formation of a specific IS competency C_j. For D_m, $m = 1, \ldots, M$; and M is the number of disciplines D_m forming the competency C_j, these weights are βk_{jm} for the levels of knowledge, βa_{jm} for the abilities, and βs_{jm} for the skills. The weights βk_{jm}, βa_{jm}, βs_{jm} are defined by experts. From our point of view for the weights' values it is easy to use 11-points range (from 0 to 10 like in Table 1 from Sect. 5). It is not so important what range the experts will choose, because while assessing the attribute values for C_j the levels KD_m, AD_m and SD_m with these weights are normalized by their sums as it is shown further (expressions (3), (4), (5)).

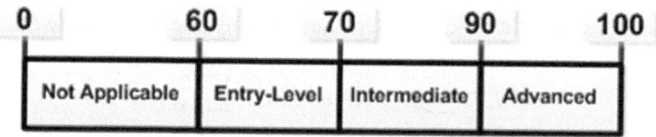

Fig. 4. Linking of scales for competency assessment

4. The single points scale from 0 to 100 is used to assess the level of competencies, their attributes and characteristics of disciplines. The transition from this scale to four-level IS competency assessment (Sect. 2) is done in accordance with Fig. 4.

The IS competencies level assessment model is shown in Fig. 5.

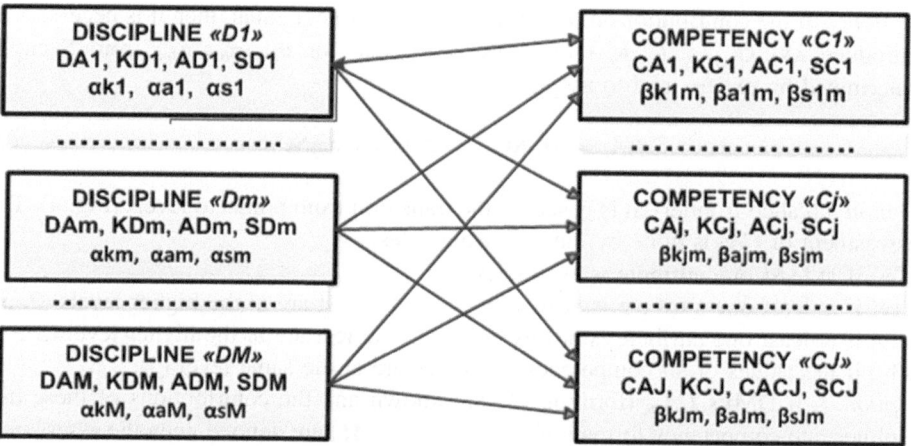

Fig. 5. Diagram of IS competencies level assessment model

Initial data for the model are the following:

1. a set of IS disciplines D_m (where $m = 1,\ldots,M; M$ is a number of disciplines), directly forming the selected IS competency C_j;
2. DML assessments DA_m $(m = 1,\ldots,M)$ and the levels KD_m, AD_m and SD_m);
3. the coefficients for each discipline $\alpha_{km}, \alpha_{am}, \alpha_{sm}$ $(m = 1,\ldots,M)$;
4. the weights βk_{jm}, βa_{jm} and βs_{jm} $(m = 1,\ldots,M)$ for attributes' assessment for C_j.

The main expressions for the model are the following.

1. Assessment of attribute value for C_j, determining the IS knowledge level:

$$KC_j = \sum_{m=1}^{M} \left(\beta k_{jm}KD_m\right) / \sum_{m=1}^{M} \left(\beta k_{jm}\right). \tag{3}$$

2. Assessment of attribute value for C_j, determining the IS abilities level:

$$AC_j = \sum_{m=1}^{M} \left(\beta a_{jm}AD_m\right) / \sum_{m=1}^{M} \left(\beta a_{jm}\right). \tag{4}$$

3. Assessment of attribute value for C_j, determining the IS skills level:

$$SC_j = \sum_{m=1}^{M} \left(\beta s_{jm} SD_m\right) / \sum_{m=1}^{M} \left(\beta s_{jm}\right). \tag{5}$$

4. Assessment of IS competency level CA_j according to the points scale. The following options are possible here.

Option 1. If the contributions of attributes into CA_j are equal, then the assessment of CA_j is calculated as:

$$CA_j = (KC_j + AC_j + SC_j)/3. \tag{6}$$

Option 2. If the contributions of attributes into CA_j are not equal, then it is necessary to introduce $\lambda k_j, \lambda a_j, \lambda s_j$ ($\lambda k_j + \lambda a_j + \lambda s_j = 1$) (like for $\alpha_{km}, \alpha_{am}, \alpha_{sm}$ from Sect. 4) determined by experts and to assess CA_j as:

$$CA_j = \lambda k_j KC_j + \lambda a_j AC_j + \lambda s_j SC_j. \tag{7}$$

Option 3 (called frontier). It is based on the transition from points to levels (Fig. 4). The assessment of CA_j is done by the following rules:
«0», if at least one attribute is at this level;
«1», if at least one attribute is at this level and the rest are at the higher levels (2, 3);
«2», if at least one attribute is at this level and the rest are at the higher level (3);
«3», if the values of all competency attributes are at the same level (3).
Option 4. If DMLs DA_m (forming C_j) are known and the contributions of these disciplines into competency formation μ_{jm} ($m = 1,\ldots,M$) are defined, then the assessment of CA_j is calculated as:

$$CA_j = \sum_{m=1}^{M} \left(\mu_{jm} DA_m\right) / \sum_{m=1}^{M} \left(\mu_{jm}\right). \tag{8}$$

If weights $\beta k_{jm}, \beta a_{jm}, \beta s_{jm}$ are defined, then values μ_{jm} can be calculated as:

$$\mu_{jm} = \beta k_{jm} + \beta a_{jm} + \beta s_{jm}. \tag{9}$$

6 Model Usage Example

The IS competencies assessment model described above is based on the system of assessing the levels of mastery of disciplines forming a specific IS competency. This model was used at the "Cybernetics and Information Security" Faculty of the National Research Nuclear University "MEPhI" (Moscow Engineering Physics Institute) (Russia) at the implementation of the "Business Continuity and Information Security Maintenance" (BC&ISM) program for Masters [5].

The requirements of the Federal State Educational Standard (FSES) of training Masters in IS were taken into account in developing the curriculum for this program.

FSES defines the area and professional activities, for which Masters should be trained. It also lists the professional activities and tasks that Masters graduates should be able to solve. The basic IS competencies are defined for each type of professional activities.

An educational institution has the right to work out its own curriculum (to choose specific disciplines) and to add more IS competencies reflecting the specific program. When a graduate masters the Masters' program, he/she will have developed additional competencies defined by the institution [5]. At the completion of training they must be able to fulfill the following activities:

- to analyze and to investigate models of systems ensuring business continuity (BC) and models of IS maintenance (C_1);
- to practically implement the standards relating to BC&ISM (C_2);
- to conduct IS risk assessment for the purpose of IS maintenance (C_3);
- to carry out the synthesis and analysis of design projects on BC&ISM for their organization where they work (O's) (C_4);
- to ensure the effective usage of O's IT resources to meet BC&ISM requirements (C_5);
- to participate in the design and operation of O's IS incident management system (C_6);
- to participate in the design and operation of O's BC&ISM system (C_7);
- to conduct technical auditing (monitoring) of O's information protection (C_8);
- to develop proposals for improving O's BC&ISM system (C_9);
- to establish and effectively implement a set of measures (rules, procedures, practical methods, guidelines, methods, tools) for BC&ISM (C_{10}).

All these competencies are developed during the implementation of a specific curriculum, which includes the specific IS disciplines [5].

The paper considers the formation of only one competency C_7 as an example, when a graduate should be able to participate in the design and operation of O's BC&ISM system.

Based on an analysis of the curriculum, ten IS disciplines D_m, $(m = 1,\ldots,M)$, form this IS competency [5]:

- 6 training courses, namely:
  - "Protected IT" (abbreviation PIT),
  - "IS Management" (ISM),
  - "IS Risk Management Basics" (ISRMB),
  - "IS Incident Management Basics" (ISIMB),
  - "IT Security Assessment" (ITSA),
  - "Business Continuity Management" (BCM),
- Practical Works during Semesters 1, 2 and 3 (P1, P2, P3), and
- Completion of a FQW (FQW).

Initial data for the IS competency assessment model are shown in Table 1. It should be noted that:

- α_{km}, α_{am}, α_{sm} for the contributions of knowledge, abilities and skills levels into the level of mastery of the particular discipline (6 training courses) were determined on

Table 1. Initial data for competency assessment modeling

D_m	T_0	T_k	T_a	T_s	α_{km}	α_{am}	α_{sm}	KD_m	AD_m	SD_m	DA_m	βk_{jm}	βa_{jm}	βs_{jm}
PIT	72	42	0	30	0,58	0	0,42	65	0	70	67	10	0	6
ISM	72	36	36	0	0,5	0,5	0	60	70	0	65	10	10	0
ISRMB	30	15	15	0	0,5	0,5	0	65	75	0	70	8	8	0
ISIMB	72	36	36	0	0,5	0,5	0	70	85	0	78	8	8	0
ITSA	72	36	36	0	0,5	0,5	0	65	65	0	65	7	6	0
BCM	32	16	16	0	0,5	0,5	0	80	85	0	83	10	10	0
P1	–	–	–	–	0,3	0,5	0,2	70	80	75	76	3	7	7
P2	–	–	–	–	0,2	0,4	0,4	70	85	80	80	2	8	8
P3	–	–	–	–	0,1	0,3	0,6	70	90	95	91	1	9	9
FQW	–	–	–	–	0,1	0,2	0,7	70	90	90	88	1	10	10

the basis of work involved in mastering the discipline (expression (2)) (T_0, T_k, T_a, T_s), taken from the curriculum [5];

- $\alpha_{km}, \alpha_{am}, \alpha_{sm}$ for the contributions of knowledge, abilities and skills levels into the level of mastery of the particular discipline (P1, P2, P3 and FQW) were determined by experts. The following peculiarities were taken into account: the contributions of the levels of gained knowledge KD_m and formed abilities AD_m decrease during the training, and the contribution of acquired skills SD_m increases;
- the levels KD_m, AD_m and SD_m were defined along a 100 point scale during progress testing (exams) for a particular student;
- the assessments of DML DA_m were determined according to the expression (1);
- the weights' values for C_7 attributes ($\beta k_{7m}, \beta a_{7m}$ and βs_{7m}) were determined by experts.

The attribute values assessments for C_7 can be determined using data from Table 1:
(1) for the knowledge level (expression (3)) $KC_7 = 68$;
(2) for the abilities level (expression (4)) $AC_7 = 76$;
(3) for the skills level (expression (5)) $SC_7 = 84$.
Within the framework of the model let us define competency C_7 level assessment CA_7 for four options.

Option 1. When the contributions of competency attributes to the level of competency is equal, then the competency level assessment will be determined by the expression (6) as $CA_7 = 76$. The competency level assessment will refer to the second (intermediate) level in accordance with the scale from Fig. 4.

Option 2. When the contribution of competency attributes to the level of competency is unequal, then it is necessary to introduce $\lambda k_7, \lambda a_7, \lambda s_7$.

If the knowledge level is more important (e.g., $\lambda k_7 = 0, 8; \lambda a_7 = 0, 1; \lambda s_7 = 0, 1$), then according to the expression (7) $CA_7 = 71$, which corresponds to the second (intermediate) level from Fig. 4.

If the abilities and skills levels are more important (e.g., $\lambda k_7 = 0, 1; \lambda a_7 = 0, 45; \lambda s_7 = 0, 45$), then according to the expression (7) $CA_7 = 79$, which also corresponds to the second (intermediate) level from Fig. 4.

Option 3. For frontier approach $CA_7 = 68$, which corresponds to the first (entry-level) level from Fig. 4.

Option 4. Using the expression (9) and data from Table 1 for $\mu_{jm}(m = 1,\ldots,M)$, it is possible to use expression (8) to determine the competency level assessment as $CA_7 = 77$, corresponding to the second (intermediate) level from Fig. 4.

7   Conclusion

The model presented in this paper allows the assessment of the level of any professional competency in the IS field. It also allows the assessment of the values of the competency's attributes according to the assessment characteristics of the disciplines that form this competency. The above example uses the model to assess one of the competencies in the IS Masters programme, confirming the usefulness and efficiency of the proposed model.

We note that using this model requires changes in the way one assesses mastery of a specific discipline. It is necessary to assess not only the entire discipline in general, but also to separately assess the levels of knowledge, abilities and skills developed by the students as they master the discipline. In addition, the values of some of the model's parameters should be determined by experts.

Approaches that have been used in this model can be applied to construct another model, which solves the inverse task. If the required IS competency level, its attributes and their assessment are known, then the actual problems are the selection and determination of the list of disciplines forming the specific competency, determination of their characteristics (the list and the level of knowledge, skills and abilities to be developed at the training completion), and formulating the initial data for a particular IS professional training curriculum and training courses. But the development of an inverse model is more complicated problem because it should use different synthesis methods. This requires solving a few optimization problems with predefined criteria.

References

1. Tolstoy, A.I.: Basis for the formation of professional competencies of graduates from educational institutions along training directions and specialities included in the enlarge direction 090000 – information security. Inf. Technol. Secur. **4**, 46–55 (2008). (in Russian)
2. Information Technology (IT) Security Essential Body of Knowledge (EBK): A Competency and Functional Framework for IT Security Workforce Development, National Cyber Security Division, United States Department of Homeland Security, October 2008
3. State Government Information Security Workforce Development Model.: A best practice model and framework, June 2010. Final Version 1.0 (US)
4. What is a Competency? http://hr.unl.edu/compensation/nuvalues/corecompetencies.shtml Accessed 22 Jan 2015
5. Miloslavskaya, N., Senatorov, M., Tolstoy, A., Zapechnikov, S.: "Business continuity and information security maintenance" masters' training program. In: Dodge Jr., R.C., Futcher, L. (eds.) WISE 6/7/8. IFIP AICT, vol. 406, pp. 95–102. Springer, Heidelberg (2013)

History of Cryptography in Syllabus on Information Security Training

Sergey Zapechnikov, Alexander Tolstoy[(⊠)], and Sergey Nagibin

The National Research Nuclear University MEPhI (Moscow Engineering Physics Institute), 31 Kashirskoye Shosse, Moscow, Russia
{SVZapechnikov, AITolstoj}@mephi.ru

Abstract. This paper discusses the peculiarities and problems of teaching the historical aspects of Information Security Science (ISS) to the students of the "Information Security" specialization. Preferential attention is given to the ISS area with the longest history, namely cryptography. We trace exactly what ideas of fundamental importance for modern cryptography were formed in each of the historical periods, how these ideas can help students in mastering the training courses' material, and how to communicate these ideas to students in the best way. The conclusions are based on the results of studies conducted over a few years at the "Cybernetics and Information Security" Faculty of the NRNU MEPhI, where our ideas are implemented in the educational process. We teach the history of cryptography in a few educational courses for Specialists in IS and Masters in Business Continuity and IS Maintenance in the form of introductory and individual lectures and seminars. Specific recommendations on the use of the historical facts considered during the classes are given.

Keywords: Information Security Science · Syllabus · Information security training · History of cryptography

1 Introduction

The study of any science's history is a part of the syllabus for students in disciplines with deep historical roots. Cryptography is one of these areas. The earliest evidence of cryptographic techniques being used for text protection refers to the XX century BC, as is well known from the archaeological data. Thus, cryptography has a history of at least forty centuries. But for a long time this area of activity was not a scientific discipline in the modern sense of the word. Rather, it was an art known to a few people who know how to protect the content of written documents from prying. Information protection (IP), and especially cryptography, began to build actively on a scientific basis only in the late XIX – early XX century. It is due to the fundamental changes in modes of representation, transmission and transformation of information in new technical systems such as the telegraph, telephone and various electromechanical devices. However, the IP method continued to be developed on the old basis until the mid XX century. The appearance of the well-known paper by Shannon, "Communication Theory of Secrecy Systems", in 1949 and the rapid development of computer technology caused an irreversible transformation of cryptography in mathematical and computer science.

© IFIP International Federation for Information Processing 2015
M. Bishop et al. (Eds.): WISE9, IFIP AICT 453, pp. 146–157, 2015.
DOI: 10.1007/978-3-319-18500-2_13

The exploration of the rich heritage of pre-scientific cryptography has a huge cognitive and wide educational value for modern IS specialists because of the abundance of ingenious solutions and good practices gained during a long quest of many generations. That makes it possible to avoid unnecessary repetition of mistakes and missteps when creating IP tools and to prevent accidents while designing cryptosystems.

Certainly, the history of science should take into account not only the history of ideas in the relevant field of expertise, but also the history of all human activities related to the implementation of these ideas. However, in a few academic disciplines it is possible to track only the most important milestones in this history, i.e. the history of ideas in the field of cryptography and other ways of document protection. The history of the facts can be traced to a much lesser extent because of the limited time allotted for the study of academic disciplines.

Therefore, it is possible to list the following reasons for including classes on the history of cryptology as a part of students' training in the field of IS:

- Such a class demonstrates that cryptography as any other significant area of human activity has not only its own theory, but its own history as well. That history helps to better understand the theory, and vice versa;
- Such a class can help students better understand how modern cryptography (and ISS in general) was formed and developed, and the laws and patterns for the accumulation and generalization of human knowledge;
- Faced with the differences and diversity of forms of man's thought and action through many centuries and countries, students can better understand their own identity and the role of modern science in historical processes.

Thus, the paper is organized as follows. After discussing the purpose of introducing the historical aspects of cryptography into the learning process in Sect. 2, we note the ways in which the history of cryptography is presented in the syllabus of training Specialists and Masters in the NRNU MEPhI. In Sects. 3–6 we discuss in more detail how the most important ideas of the main periods in cryptography development (pre-scientific, classical science, transition phase from classical to modern science and modern science) can best be taught by the lecturers and studied by the students of a few courses on IS. Section 7 briefly presents some related works. The directions of future work are identified in conclusion.

2 Forms of History of Cryptography's Classes

In accordance with the state Russian educational standards, courses training Specialists and Masters do not discuss the history of science. The "History and Methodology of Science" discipline is provided only for post-graduate students. In this regard, we have to look for other ways to have the students learn about the history of the field of science in the process of mastering the syllabus. Some ways are:

- introductory lectures on various subjects;
- scientific seminars;

- individual lectures on the "Humanitarian Issues of Information Security" and "Cryptographic Protocols and Standards" disciplines for the Specialists in IS;
- lectures and workshops as a part of the introductory discipline entitled "Fundamentals of Business Continuity and Information Security Maintenance" for the Masters.

Presenting history in the introductory lectures allows the instructor to place the studied disciplines into their general scientific context, to show communications and parallels with the other disciplines, including those devoted to the study of almost exclusively classical science such as basic mathematical and engineering disciplines. For example, it is very useful to draw a time axis with the major periods in the history of cryptography and to show the development of different areas of this science at the second half of the XX century at the introductory lecture on the "Cryptographic Protocols and Standards" discipline (Fig. 1).

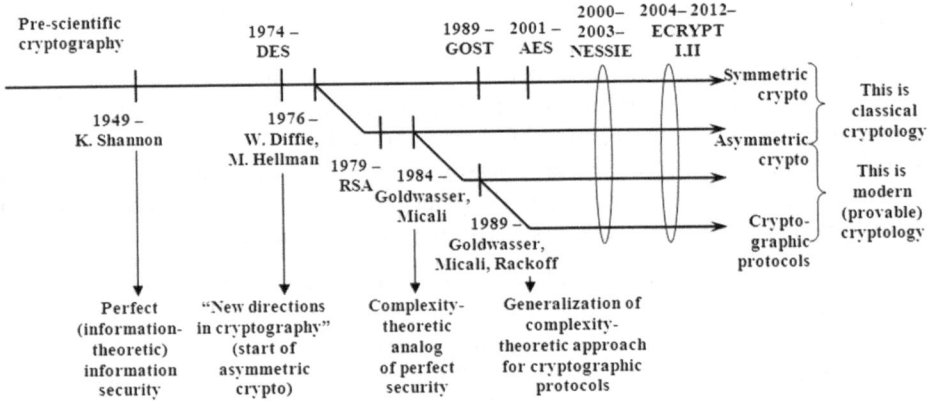

Fig. 1. Scheme's example used during the introductory lecture to the "Cryptographic Protocols and Standards" discipline, showing cryptography's history periodization

Our experience shows that the teachers of classes on the history of cryptography should have a good knowledge not only in the world history, but also in the foundations of cryptography. Since the classes are designed for the students specializing in mathematical and computer sciences, it is better that the teachers' basic education is natural or computer sciences rather than humanitarian sciences.

We recommend seminars in an interactive form. For example, all students take turns preparing reports, discussing them with their teachers and presenting them during the classes. The necessary requirements for getting credits for that part of an educational course that includes one section on the history of cryptography are their own report presentation, reviewing 2–3 reports of other students, and participating in their discussions.

In general, while planning the history of cryptography classes, we divide the history into the following periods:

I. Pre-scientific period (from ancient times to the end of the XVII century);

II. Classical science period, in which the scientific basis of cryptography was formed (XVIII–XIX centuries);

III. Transition phase from classical to modern science (the end of the XIX century – the beginning of the XX century); and

IV. Modern cryptography (the second half of the XX century – the beginning of the XXI century).

The history of related sciences (e.g. steganography and methods of protection against falsification of paper documents and banknotes) is also discussed in parallel with the history of cryptography, using the same periods.

Some recommendations for the study of the main periods in the history of cryptography, as well as a few ideas that can be implemented during lectures and seminars, are presented in the following sections.

3 The Pre-scientific Period and Its Lessons

The main educational reason for studying the pre-scientific period of cryptography's development is to show the following:

- what main methodological ideas were used in the first known techniques of cryptographic IP;
- how these ideas were developed and generalized as time passed; and
- why they continue to be the foundation of many cryptographic techniques.

This period is illuminated in a number of books on the history of cryptography [1–5]. However, in most modern textbooks on cryptographic IP methods the pre-scientific period's codes serve only as a background against which to present the advanced modern techniques. However, research into the ancient techniques of protecting written communications still cannot be considered completed. The codes used in ancient Greece, ancient Rome, and medieval Western Europe are well-known and described in detail. They overshadow the achievements of many other nations and civilizations that also contribute to the history of cryptography. Therefore, when creating material for our classes, we use not only well-known sources, but also rely on the results of our own research [6–8].

The ancient and medieval methods of protecting written texts are very suitable to demonstrate to the students the basic principles of concealing the text contents from unauthorized persons, as well as the simplest methods of their breaking. The main difference between them and modern ciphers is simplicity meaning that they are easily observable. The basic ideas can be easily explained by the teacher during one lecture and can be understood even by those students who do not specialize in the field of IS or other areas of mathematical and computer sciences.

However, the teacher should be cautioned against too direct a comparison of pre-scientific and modern IP methods. Ancient cryptography should be considered primarily a linguistic phenomenon and a specific method of transmitting thoughts by a community of people, knowing one or another "secret language". Its main feature compared to modern cryptography is that the text was merely a sequence of characters, regardless of its semantic content (coherent text, a set of numbers, etc.), whereas modern cryptography is based on mathematical formalism and formal logic.

In this regard, we recommend the teacher emphasize the following while discussing cryptography of the prescientific period.

1. Almost all ancient civilizations knew cryptography as a special linguistic phenomenon, fixing on physical media the "secret languages" that existed in different social groups since time immemorial. These languages have an origin in magical ritual, but later they were understood as a tool for social communication. In this regard, cryptography has two main application areas in the ancient history:

   - "magic" – to conceal a meaning of names, magic rituals, secret ritual knowledge and another taboo information, i.e. for secret communications with the supernatural (that was an integral part of the lives of all ancient civilizations);
   - "practical" – to protect military reports, personal correspondence, and perhaps trade secrets, i.e. for secret communication in human society.

2. The most important encryption principles – replacement and permutation of characters – were empirically discovered in the Ancient World. In the Ancient World, these principles exhausted the arsenal of cryptographic protection methods for written texts, and they were realized only for special, very simple cases. Evolution of the cryptographic methods was extremely slow because the existing methods were generally sufficient.

3. Along with cryptography, the ancient civilizations used various methods of physical protection of messages by encoding and steganography. That served different practical purposes such as concealing the fact of message's existence or transfer, hiding the names of senders or recipients, accelerating copying text and reducing the amount of material to be carried or memorized, transmitting messages at a rate greater than a man's speed, and raising the value of the text to the reader. These objectives were often seen as a priority compared to concealing the message's meaning from unauthorized persons.

While studying cryptography in the Middle Ages and the early New Ages (XVI – XVII centuries) it is reasonable to stress the following:

- The encryption methods have become more complex in the Middle Ages: polyalphabetic substitution has been invented. The systematic methods of cryptanalysis have appeared in the Arabian world for the first time;
- Signatures and stamps ensured a document's authenticity for the first time in Byzantium, along with encryption ensuring the confidentiality of documents;
- Ciphers are still considered a linguistic phenomenon: single words, sentences, paragraphs, sections of the document are converted.

One of the techniques that can be used to indicate a close relationship between history and modernity of cryptography and to inspire students who are accustomed to think in terms of modern mathematics and formal logic is to mathematically analyze ancient ciphers (like shift, replacement, affine and permutation ciphers). However, the general cases of substitutions and (or) permutation were not implemented in any classical ciphers and cryptographic devices, and the particular cases used essentially reduce the cipher strength. Nevertheless, a number of examples might illustrate the fact that the most secure classic ciphers such as the Vigenère cipher and "Latin squares" are widely regarded as almost unbreakable until the appearance of computers in the XX century.

Our experience shows that the students analyze classical ciphers with great interest. On the one hand, the examples are readily understandable and the validity of the findings can be checked without using software. On the other hand, similar analysis of the modern ciphers' security such as AES, the Russian standard GOST 28147-89 [9], RC6, etc. is simply impossible in classes because of great complexity of ciphers and the time required.

4 The Period of Classical Science

The main educational goal in studying the period of classical science is to show how the important mathematical methods were formed during this period. They have become the basis of a variety of protection methods (including asymmetric cryptography) later in the XX century. Many discoverers cannot anticipate the fundamental importance of their works for the future of science.

The classical science period (the XVI century – the end of the XIX century) is a stage of historical development of science, during which the system of the most important natural science concepts and ideas was formed. This system is the foundation of today's scientific knowledge and method. Mathematical knowledge particularly flourished during this period. This is fully applicable to cryptography. Many famous scientists can be mentioned here: Leon Battista Alberti, Francois Vieta, Giovanni Battista Porta, Blaise de Vigenère, Francis Bacon, as well as many interesting ciphers' designs of the time: Cardan grille, Vigenère's cipher and many others. Research about this period of cryptography's development has not been completed. Therefore, while creating lessons for the classes we used our own scientific results [10].

During the classes, we draw students' attention to the following basic ideas related to the period of classical science:

- Encryption techniques become more complicated: combinations of substitutions and permutations in one cipher are used;
- Methods of cryptanalysis are improved and a competition between cryptographers and cryptanalysts is enhanced;
- Pure and applied mathematics, long considered just an abstraction, are developed; later in the XX century they served as the foundation for most of the natural sciences and engineering; and
- Principles of engineering and technical IP begin to be developed as one of the areas of engineering science.

Our experience shows that one of the most effective forms of studying the classical science's period is to obtain an acquaintance with the biographies of the outstanding scientists who greatly contributed to the mathematical foundations of modern cryptography and its creative and scientific methods.

The most striking example that should be included in the syllabus is a study of Leonard Euler's creative heritage. Euler's contribution to world science is truly priceless. He essentially founded several mathematical sciences: analytic number theory, calculus of variations, complex function theory, differential geometry of surfaces, analytical mechanics, rigid body dynamics, as well as many parts of the theory of differential equations, theory of algorithms, theory of elliptic functions, celestial mechanics and other areas of pure and applied mathematics. This scientist had encyclopedic knowledge. His interests extended to many branches of astronomy, acoustics, optics, statistics, botany, medicine, chemistry, linguistics, music, and engineering. Almost all Euler's results belonging to the areas of mathematics that form the foundations of modern cryptology are centered on his discoveries in numbers theory.

At present Euler's works are considered to be the most important and fundamental works for asymmetric cryptography. Of course, Euler himself could not have foreseen the development of the methods and areas of cryptology known today and studied in different courses as the basis of this science. However, the main ways of using Euler's results can be grouped into four categories:

1. Testing the primality of numbers (widely used to generate asymmetric cryptographic parameters);
2. Computationally complex problems in number theory (e.g. the Euler theorem, study of the properties of quadratic residues and the theory of primitive roots; these are closely related to three computationally complex problems in numbers theory, which now form the basis of the most common asymmetric cryptosystems, namely the Rivest-Shamira-Adleman (RSA) problem, the problem of quadratic residues and the discrete logarithm problem);
3. Cryptosystems based on computationally complex problems. The RSA problem is the basis of security of the RSA encryption scheme and the RSA digital signature scheme. Security of cryptosystems such as the Goldwasser-Micali probabilistic open encryption scheme, the pseudo-random BBS (Blum-Blum-Shub) generator and the Paillier open encryption scheme is based on the problem of quadratic residues. The ElGamal encryption scheme and the ElGamal digital signature scheme and its variants DSA (USA digital signature standard) and GOST R 34.10-2012 (Russian digital signature standard) [11] are based on the discrete logarithm problem; and
4. Cryptographic protocols that use primitives based on the above computationally complex problems. Some constructions, the security of which is based on the same computationally complex problems, can be used in addition to the above listed cryptosystems as the building blocks for cryptographic protocols. The most famous example is the Diffie-Hellman public key distribution protocol and numerous protocols derived from it (e.g. MTI, STS, etc.). Their security is ultimately based on the discrete logarithm problem and the Diffie-Hellman problem. Less well-known examples are the zero-knowledge proof protocols that can use all three of the above problems. For example, security of the Shnorr zero-knowledge authentication scheme is based on the intractabilility of the discrete logarithm problem.

The above examples are enough to make a conclusion about the fundamental significance of Euler's results for modern cryptologic science. The most important results, which seemed during his lifetime to be a game of numbers, have provided the mathematical basis for asymmetric cryptography two hundred years after Euler's death.

Another set of no less spectacular examples that can be discussed in the classroom are the biographies of the great German mathematician Carl Gauss and the brilliant French mathematician Evariste Galois, both far ahead of their time in the creation of group theory and the theory of finite fields.

5 The Transition Phase from Classical to Modern Science

From our point of view, the main educational goal of studying the transition phase from classical to modern science is to become familiar with the concepts that became the basis of "new" cryptography at that time. Scientific and technological progress leads to changes in presentation and communication of information, and formation of the most important concepts such as data (as information provided in a computer form), coding (as a system of rules of information transfer in the data), etc. This is due, primarily, to the development of the telegraph, telephone, and electromechanical devices of information transforming.

Thus, during the classes on the history of cryptography it is necessary to identify and explain to the students the following basic ideas related to this period:

- There was a fundamental change in media, the ways of presenting, processing, and transmitting information such as electrical signals and electromechanical machines, replace paper and pencil in this period;
- The perfectly secret cipher was invented in 1917 (by Vernam of the AT&T company), but its perfect secrecy was justified intuitively – that property was not strictly proven for the cipher;
- Construction principles for the ciphers used in practice evolved nearly to modern principles; codes' design became a complex network of substitutions and permutations, but they were realized by means of the mechanical and electromagnetic devices available at that time; and
- Both block and stream ciphers were widely applied in practice.

From our point of view, it is appropriate for the classes to include some materials primarily related to the invention of the one-time cipher pad and the rotor cipher machines.

It is well known that Gilbert Sandford Vernam invented the automated one-time pad (perfectly secret cipher) in 1917. Studying the one-time pad is usually included in the curriculum of the standard cryptologic educational courses. Therefore, to avoid repetition it should be used as a basis to draw parallels with more recent inventions in the field of cryptography as well as to show a specific example of how new discoveries appear as a result of generalization of known results and, in turn, how former discoveries become the special cases of new discoveries. The one-time pad is very useful for that purpose as the inventor of the cipher assumed that it is unbreakable without proving that fact.

The mathematical formulation of the problem of IP, and derivation of the ideal conditions under which its solution is possible, was developed by C.Shannon (1949) [12]. Shannon's theory implies that the Vernam cipher is a special case that provides information-theoretic but not practical security. Thus, more than 30 years passed between an invention with an intuitively reasonable argument, and the rigorous proof of that argument.

However, this date does not mark the end of the history associated with the invention of the one-time pad. At the beginning of the 1980s G.R. Blakley has shown [13] that the Vernam cipher is just a special case of the so-called shadow ciphers.

In addition, with the discovery of the threshold cryptography principle by A. Shamir [14], it became possible to assert that the Vernam cipher is a special case of the threshold secret sharing schemes, namely a 2.2 Asmuth-Bloom threshold secret sharing scheme.

The study of this example helps the students understand better the typical path of development of scientific knowledge from the particular to the general.

The history of the creation and cryptanalysis of perhaps the most famous families of the rotor cipher machines can be used during the classes to illustrate the period. The lecture should note that the rotor cipher machines are already the direct prototypes of the modern block and stream ciphers, implementing the same principles: layered substitution and permutation transforms for the block ciphers and pseudo-random generator for the stream ciphers. The German Enigma machines, the American Hagelin machines (M-209, C-52 etc.) and the Russian Fialka M-125 machines implemented block ciphers. The German Lorenz SZ 40 and SZ 42 machines implemented the stream ciphers.

It is appropriate to discuss a mathematical description of a rather complex transformation implemented by the rotor cipher machines, and a mathematical formulation of the inverse cryptanalytic problem of finding a transformation key. The teacher can ask the students to conduct their own assessment of the algorithm's complexity. Doing so will allow them to get a clear idea of how much more difficult the problem is while comparing it with cryptanalysis of the pre-scientific ciphers, and why the creation of the first computers by the group under Alan Turing supervision was required to solve it.

The software models of some rotor cipher machines presented on the Internet (for example, a good simulator of Hagelin's M-209 machine [15]) can be used here for illustrative purposes.

Finally, to complete the study of the period it is necessary to characterize Shannon's works and above all his famous "Communication Theory of Secrecy Systems" [12] as well as the works of his followers. It should be emphasized that the essential impact of this Shannon's work is that he formulated the idea of information-theoretic secrecy.

The IS concept as a philosophical concept was formulated in the same period. N.J. Danilevsky (1822–1885) was the first Russian scientists to address the problem [16]. Our colleagues developed it further in [17].

6 Studying Modern Cryptography

While studying the history of modern cryptography it should be stressed that the subject of cryptography expanded and became one of the computer sciences, along with the other sciences like the theory of algorithms, programming, the computational complexity theory, etc. The history of its development becomes a part of the IT history. Various computer equipment, information, and telecommunications systems provide the technical basis for the implementation of all basic IP methods and tools. The largest manufacturers of IT products, leading universities, and research centers became the driving force behind the development of ISS.

In addition to paper, new media in the form of a global, distributed, electronic environment for information processing appeared. New "computer" cryptography with its two main branches (symmetric and asymmetric) becomes the basis of most, if not all IP methods.

Modern cryptography almost entirely focuses on the computer processing of information and the development of appropriate algorithmic and technical methods. Works devoted to new methods of securing information using paper as well as encryption algorithms that can be executed manually are few in number.

It should be taken into account that the study of many important discoveries of the second half of the XX century is usually included in standard courses on cryptography. To avoid repetition, we recommend the teacher focus on the personalities and companies that greatly contributed to the development of IS science and practice. In this case, a good example is the history of the highest award in the field of Computer Science and IT – the Turing Award, often called the "Nobel Prize of computing". Five outstanding scientists in the field of mathematical foundations of cryptography, formal and logical methods of IS and related fields have been rewarded over the past 20 years [18]: Manuel Blum, Andrew Yao, Ronald Rivest, Silvio Micali and Shafi Goldwasser, and Leslie Lamport. They are well known to those skilled in IS. These facts indicate that IS is recognized by the community of scientists as an extremely important area of modern computer science.

During the classes we also recommend giving the students an idea of the work of the cryptographic community, which fundamentally changed in the second half of the XX century. Cryptography is no longer a "secret" science. The perception is that the chance of finding a solution that is stable, free from faults and weaknesses is much higher when an open and comprehensive discussion of new cryptosystems occurs by the whole scientific community. In recent decades, this kind of activity mainly goes through a process of international (and national) standardization.

As an example of the results brought by standardization and its problems, the teacher can mention the development and adoption of the first USA encryption standard DES (1979), the first Russian encryption standard GOST 28147-89 (1989) [9], the new USA encryption standard AES (2001), other USA cryptography standards such as FIPS 140, SHA, DSA, the widely-used international cryptography standard ISO/IEC 18033 (2006–2010), new Russian standards GOST 34.10-2012 (elliptic curve digital signature) [11] and GOST R 34.11-2012 (hash function Streebog) [19], etc.

Another aspect of the history of cryptography is the historiography of cryptography and cryptanalysis. During the second half of the XX century, a number of fundamental works on the history of cryptography from ancient times to the present days appeared. Of course, the greatest impact on the public has been Kahn's book "The Codebreakers: The Story of Secret Writing" [1]. It initiated a number of other works and in general significantly increased interest in the history of cryptography and cryptanalysis. Many researchers around the world began to study their national traditions and achievements of their countries in the field of cryptography in different epochs.

7 Related Works

Of course, we are not the only ones to include historical aspects of ISS in the students' syllabus. The history of ISS and in particular the history of cryptography is not often highlighted as a separate academic discipline (course), but some sections of "Cryptography" or "Network Security" disciplines, dedicated to the history of cryptography, are taught in several Russian and foreign universities. In particular, a section on the history of cryptography is included in the online "Cryptography I" course by Dan Boneh at the "Coursera" portal [20]. Some other universities worldwide have specific courses on the history of cryptography [21–23], including Russian universities [24].

8 Conclusion

Summarizing the results of introducing the history of cryptography into the syllabus for the students' training on IS direction, we conclude with the following.

1. Studying the history of cryptography serves one of the essential aspects of forming the professional expertise for students preparing to become an IS specialist or the Masters in Business Continuity and Information Security Maintenance.
2. Studying the history of cryptography allows the students to deeply understand why ISS has developed the way it has. The theory cannot explain everything; some issues are due to traditions. And this leads to a deeper understanding of the subject.
3. Knowing the history allows to understand the current trends and predict the future.

Most of our findings are original; they are based on our own investigations of the history of cryptography. We are going to continue this research in order to create a tutorial, which will reflect adequately all periods of cryptologic science, with particular attention to the development of this branch of knowledge in Russia. Any historical research is always laborious and requires a long time, but we hope to report the results of our new research in this area at the next WISE10 conference.

References

1. Kahn, D.: The Codebreakers: The Story of Secret Writing. Macmillan, New York (1967)
2. Mollin, R.: Codes: The Guide to Secrecy from Ancient to Modern Times. Taylor & Francis Group, Abingdon (2005)

3. Bauer, F.: Decrypted Secrets: Methods and Maxims of Cryptology, 4th edn. Springer, Heidelberg (2007)
4. Rusetskaya, I.A.: Istoriya kriptografii v Zapadnoy Evrope v rannee novoe vremya. Universitetskaya kniga, Sankt-Peterburg, Tsentr gumanitarnyh initsiativ (2014). (in Russian)
5. Bauer, C.: Secret History: The Story of Cryptology. CRC Press, Boca Raton (2013)
6. Zapechnikov, S.V.: Cryptography as the phenomenon of Russian literature language (XII–XVII centuries). Secur. Inf. Technol. **2**, 116–123 (2011). (in Russian)
7. Zapechnikov, S.V.: Protection of documents, cryptography and secret communications in Byzantium (IV–XV centuries). Secur. Inf. Technol. **2**, 49–61 (2012). (in Russian)
8. Zapechnikov, S.V.: Cryptography and secret communications in the Ancient world. Secur. Inf. Technol. **2**, 83–95 (2014). (in Russian)
9. Russian state encryption standard GOST 28147-89. http://en.wikipedia.org/wiki/GOST_ (block_cipher)
10. Zapechnikov, S.V.: About the history of cryptography: the Leonardo Euler's contribution in formation of mathematical basis for modern cryptology. Herald of Russian State University of Humanities: Informatics. Inf. Secur. **14**(94), 29–52 (2012). (in Russian)
11. Russian state digital signature standard GOST R 34.10-2012. https://tools.ietf.org/html/draft-dolmatov-gost34102012-00
12. Shannon, C.: Communication theory of secrecy systems. http://netlab.cs.ucla.edu/wiki/files/shannon1949.pdf
13. Blakley, G.R.: Key management from a security viewpoint. Advances in cryptography – A report on CRYPTO'81. ECE Rept No 82-04, Department of Electrical and Computer Engineering, University of California, Santa Barbara, CA, USA, pp. 82 (1982)
14. Shamir, A.: How to share a secret. Comm. ACM. **22**, 612–613 (1979)
15. US M-209 Simulator 3.0. http://users.telenet.be/d.rijmenants/en/m209sim.htm
16. Danilevsky, N.J.: Russia and Europe. Kniga, Moscow (1991). (in Russian)
17. Malyuk, A., Miloslavskaya, N.: Information security theory development. In: Proceedings of the 7th International Conference on Security of Information and Networks (SIN2014). 9–11 September 2014, Glasgow, UK, pp. 52–55. ACM, New York (2014)
18. "Turind Award" at Wikipedia. http://en.wikipedia.org/wiki/Turing_Award
19. Russian state hash function algorithm GOST R 34.11-2012. https://tools.ietf.org/html/rfc6986
20. Boneh, D.: "Cryptography" online course. https://www.coursera.org/course/crypto
21. History of computer cryptography and secrecy systems. http://www.dsm.fordham.edu/~mathai/crypto.html
22. Cryptography defined/brief history. http://www.laits.utexas.edu/~anorman/BUS.FOR/course.mat/SSim/history.html
23. Cryptography: The private history of secret codes. https://brooklynbrainery.com/courses/cryptography-the-private-history-of-secret-codes
24. "History of cryptography" course at Higher School of Economics. http://www.hse.ru/edu/courses/126240458.html (in Russian)

Author Index